# IN THE ALTOGETHER

Trusting God with All We Hide From the World

**TAYLOR JOHNSON**

ISBN:978-1-7334290-0-9

To the body of Christ

# CONTENTS

# INTRODUCTION

You could have sworn the invitation said this was a costume party.

Clearly, you were wrong, and you see that now as you walk through the front door. All of your friends in their regular clothes. Uh oh. If your face weren't covered in elaborate special effects make-up, everyone would be able to see how red you were turning. That's the one silver lining: no one can tell when a Dracula gets embarrassed.

What would you do in that scenario? You're the only one at a party wearing a costume, and you have a few options on how to handle this embarrassing situation. If you were a real Dracula, you could just turn into a bat and fly away. Would you ride it out even though you look ridiculous in a sea of regular people?

It would be even worse if you didn't know everyone at the party. Like if it was a friend of a friend's house. For everyone else, this would be their first impression of you. The rest of your life, they'd remember you as the weird Dracula who showed up in full costume to a stranger's engagement party.

Can you imagine how bizarre it would be for the exact opposite situation to happen?

You could have sworn the invitations didn't say anything about costumes. You should know, you made them yourself. This is your party, and you never intended for it to be a costume party, and yet here are all of your guests, every single one of them in costume. You're the only one dressed as yourself. What's even more bizarre is that no one is acting like themselves. Everyone is staying in character, acting like the person they dressed up as. The guy in the firefighter costume is pretending he's a real firefighter, the Jedi is acting like a real Jedi, and the guy in the E.T. costume will not stop talking like E.T. No one will have a real conversation with you. No one is willing to drop the act.

If this happened to me, I'm sure at first I'd be baffled. I might even find it a little funny. Is this a prank? A dream? It's too bizarre to be real.

It wouldn't take long, though, for the shock to wear off and frustration to take over. This is not the party I wanted to have. I was hoping to have genuine conversations with my friends. I invited these people because I wanted to connect with them, but it's impossible when no one is willing to drop the act. I'm sure the only time anyone would break character would be for an emergency. If Darth Vader clogs the toilet, he doesn't have time to do the impression. He needs help so he'd come over to me as himself.

It would make for a terrible party.

I wonder if this is what it's like to be Jesus with the church. He's invited us into His home, not just as friends but as newly adopted members of His family. Even though it was nowhere on the invitation, we tend to show up in costume, never breaking character, pretending to be this perfect version of ourselves. There's no way to connect with us because we refuse to be real.

What's missing from the party is a willingness to be vulnerable. To get rid of your costume is to make yourself vulnerable. Your guard is down, your true self is exposed. The good and the bad are out in the open. In a room full of people still in character, it's risky to be yourself, so we save it only for emergencies. A lot of the time in the church vulnerability is seen as a last resort. Once you've tried everything else on your own, none of it working, then you can try talking to someone else about it. Maybe. We'll see. Opening up is only for when you hit rock bottom.

We have too narrow a view of vulnerability.

This is not how the church was designed to work.

Costumes were never on the invitation.

Vulnerability was never meant for special occasions, but that's how we treat it. If we think that not everyone needs to open up about what's going on in their lives, then we can turn it into an event. You get one or two chances a year. We schedule these rare moments where a pastor gets up and says, *Alright! If you've got something going on and you need to break character, now's your chance.* When you're a teenager growing up in church, you might have to wait for that one night of youth camp where everyone gets to talk about their baggage. If you're an adult, it might be at a conference or a retreat. Maybe it's never at all. When the scheduled event is over, you feel like you've missed your chance. You'll have to wait for whenever the next one comes around. That's how I felt for the longest time.

I grew up in church. From junior high, all the way through college, I had no idea how to deal with depression or anxiety, and I was too scared to tell anyone about it. I did my best to push those feelings down and never let them out. There were times I experimented with self-harm and other moments I got very close to taking my own life. Those special occasions would show up every once in a while at church, but I could never work up the courage to break character. It was too big of a secret. I was terrified that if I came out from behind my costume and showed what was really going on with me, people would never look at me the same again. My life would be ruined.

My insecurities led me to believe I was the only one actually wearing a costume. Everyone else really was as perfect as they presented themselves.

I know there are other people with that same fear. They too sit quietly in church services and small groups, keeping relationships shallow because they can only go so deep when they're in character. They're suffering in silence, too frightened of what may come if they speak up.

Still, others have forgotten they're even wearing a costume. They've said *I'm fine* so many times they actually believe it. Often the picture we paint of who needs to be vulnerable is just small enough that we don't fit in the frame. We get to escape.

4

We can stay in the safety of our costume. It's just for people whose lives are *really* falling apart. The rest of us don't need to let people in. No one needs to know our past, our home life, our fears, our regrets, or our dreams. We don't have to share what we're praying for or what God's dealing with us about. We think because things aren't that bad, we're allowed to pretend we're perfect.

That's just not true.

Vulnerability is a part of the foundation of what it means to follow Christ.

Jesus' invitation into His family is also an invitation to strip away the costumes we feel we must wear with the rest of the world. This book is called *In the Altogether*, which is an old-timey phrase that means to be naked. That's precisely what vulnerability feels like. It's scary. It's risky. You're fully uncovered, and people can see ALL of you. You're revealing the most sensitive parts of yourself. It's terrifying to be naked in front of someone, especially if you don't know how they're going to react.

Can you imagine having to strip down in front of your doctor and the moment they see you, they scream and jump out the window? What if you just got married and the first time your spouse saw you naked they laughed until they threw up? That sounds awful. That would ruin you for life. If that's the risk I'm taking, it might be safer to stay covered up forever.

But Jesus died in our place to defeat the shame that causes us to hide behind a costume. Christ came to establish the kingdom of heaven, a community where there is freedom to live emotionally and spiritually in the altogether. If we can expand the way we think about vulnerability, that it's not just for rock bottom, but a part of our everyday lives, it can bring such incredible change to the church.

It can change how we approach community.

It can change the way we deal with sin.

It can help us fight loneliness.

When the church is full of people who are willing to be fully known for who they really are, it brings new life to a boring party. Think of all the reasons you've heard people give for leaving the church.

*Everyone is super fake.*

*I didn't feel like I fit in.*

*The church is full of hypocrites.*

Those are valid reasons. A church that understands the role vulnerability plays in the life of a Christian can show a new hope to those who have walked away.

I want to show you why vulnerability is critical, what it looks like in the life of the church, why we're afraid of it (it's terrifying!), and why we don't have to be.

But first I have to convince you we don't have to be afraid to even talk about this stuff. The kind of self-examination that comes along with a topic like this can be really uncomfortable. Being honest with yourself isn't always easy. Trust me, I know. I avoided being vulnerable for the longest time because I was afraid of what was waiting for me outside my comfort zone.

My whole life, the thing that has made it easier to approach uncomfortable topics is humor. It's not just because I've been a stand-up comedian for over a decade, but because of the way I was raised. Growing up, I rarely saw my parents disagree (argue) without them also making each other laugh. Comedy disarms you. It brings down your walls.

When my dad was diagnosed with Alzheimer's, one of the first things he told my mom was that he still wanted to make jokes about it. If you can laugh, you're not afraid. It's not bigger than you. If you can laugh about it, you can talk about it. That's still true in my family. There are times when the family is all together for a holiday, my dad goes to say something, and he gets lost mid-thought. There's a long, awkward pause. The room grows still with this unspoken tension as we all silently root for him to find his footing in his own mind again. In those moments, my dad can still crack a joke. It's his way of taking power away from the disease. Every time we laugh, we shrink the elephant in the room to a more manageable size. We don't have to tiptoe around it. If we can laugh, we can talk.

That's why I love being a comedian.

That's why I end my shows with a message.

That's why this book is going to be full of the most ridiculous embarrassing stories.

If we can laugh about our fear of vulnerability, we can talk about it.

And there's a lot we need to talk about.

# CHAPTER 1

# DECIDING WHO YOU WANT TO BE

*[On Authenticity]*

"If you're loved by someone, you're never rejected
Decide what to be and go be it"

The Avett Brothers

There's this Diet Coke commercial I think is garbage.

Gillian Jacobs—a very funny actress who doesn't deserve any blame for this terrible commercial—is walking out of a store and down the street as she talks to the camera. Here's what she says:

Look, here's the thing about Diet Coke—

OK. We're already off to a bad start. Never start a sentence with "look." It's unnecessary unless you're asking me to literally look at something. "Look at that falcon trying to steal a baby!" Great. Yes. Perfect use of the word. That is something I'm interested in seeing.

If you're trying to convince me of something and you start with "look" you've already lost me. It's impossible to say it without a condescending tone.

Try it. Say "look" in the kindest, sweetest, friendliest tone. It's impossible.

I feel the same way about the phrase "here's the thing." You can't say that without sounding rude either. Here's THE thing? You have the one, central, absolute thing about this subject that is going to change my mind? How do you know that with such certainty? There are so many things. How do you know THE ONE?!

Also, this is such a strange way to start a commercial. It's like we're opening in the middle of an argument I don't remember starting. Why is this commercial trying to fight me? What did I ever do to hurt you, Diet Coke? I don't want any trouble. I also don't want a Diet Coke. I'll take a Dr Pepper.

Let's start over.

> Here's the thing about Diet Coke: It's delicious.
> It makes me feel good.

No. Stop. This sounds so unnatural. I've never heard someone say Diet Coke makes them feel good. Naps make me feel good. A hug from a loved one makes me feel good. Making people laugh feels good. Saving a baby from a wild falcon feels good. You want me to believe diet soda belongs on that list? If I was hanging out with a friend, and they said, "DIET COKE MAKES ME FEEL GOOD!" I wouldn't believe them. They were paid to say that or they're an alien.

> Life is short.

You're right. I could die at any moment. I don't want the last thing I hear before I pass to be, "Diet Coke is delicious."

> If you want to live in a yurt—

This is where the commercial goes off the rails.

—Yurt it up!

I don't even know what that is, but I'm disgusted.

If you want to run a marathon—I mean, that sounds SUPER hard but—OK.

Wait. What is happening here? It sounds like Diet Coke doesn't believe in me. Do they think I'm too lazy to run a marathon?

I mean, just do you, whatever that is. And if you're in the mood for a Diet Coke, have a Diet Coke.

What's so funny is that a commercial that is essentially about authenticity ends up coming across so inauthentic. Diet Coke is trying really hard to sound so cool, but it sounds like it was written by an undercover cop. It feels forced and disingenuous. *Yo kids, it's me your BFF Diet Coke! You don't have to listen to anyone else. When you drink Diet Coke, it means you're being yourself and doing whatever you feel like! Now watch me do this skateboard trick and remember to stay in school!*

I understand why Diet Coke would want a commercial with this message. Our current culture is obsessed with authenticity. Everybody seems to be very concerned with being their most authentic self. It's one of the biggest compliments you can pay someone: *You're just really authentic. I love how you're not afraid to be yourself.* We want to look within and find the truth that's been inside us all along. It's in our movies, our music, our Diet Coke commercials, and our books.

I searched Amazon for the word authentic, and I found an avalanche of books like:

*\* Authentic: How to be yourself and why it matters*

*\* Authentic Happiness: Using the new positive psychology to realize your potential for lasting fulfillment*

*\* Authentic Christianity: How Lutheran Theology Speaks to a Postmodern World*

*\* Authentic Leadership: Rediscovering the Secrets to Creating Lasting Value*

If we're not careful, and overemphasize its importance, the push for authenticity can cause a lot of damage. Left unchecked, we can stunt our growth, limit relationships, and can convince ourselves we don't need vulnerability. That's a hard thing for me to say because I know the value of the message. Over the years, it's helped me become comfortable in my own skin. This showed itself in a few different areas.

I'm an introvert. This can surprise people who have only seen me on stage because I can get loud and crazy when performing. After shows, I'll meet people and hang out, but eventually, I need to be alone. I love to travel and speak, but I need to make sure I have some quiet alone time because I can get so drained.

Susan Cain, author of *Quiet: The Power of Introverts in a World that Can't Stop Talking,* spoke to a massive misconception about introverts in her TED Talk. "[Being an introvert] is different from being shy. Shyness is about fear of social judgment. Introversion is about how you respond to stimulation."[1] For some people, all of the stimulation of being in a crowd is just what they need to recharge. That's where they thrive. If they go too long without being around people, it can affect their mood.

Introverts, on the other hand, need to get away from the stimulation and find a quiet place to recover. I had no idea this was what was happening with me whenever I'd hang out with a lot of people. I don't know if I even understood what an introvert was.

I'd make myself stay at parties long after I had been thoroughly drained because I thought that was what I was supposed to do. It's not like I was having fun forcing myself to stick around. I'd be quiet, miserable, and probably rude. People would pressure me to go out with them, saying things like, "Come on, Taylor! Don't be a party pooper! You've got to come!" But once I was there, I'm sure they were thinking, "We've made a huge mistake. How do we get this guy out of here?" Nothing ruins a party like a crabby introvert.

I'm so thankful I understand myself better now. I'm glad I can tell when I need to spend some time alone. It's better for everyone this way. I'm thankful for friends who understand too. While we're all together I can say, "I need to go for a quick walk," and no one questions it. They know.

No one says, "What? Why? What's wrong with you? Why are you being weird? Just hang out!"

In her TED Talk, Cain explains how often in our culture, we hold up the characteristics of extroverts as if they're the ultimate ideal. We think this is how everyone should act; this is what we should all hope to be. That's the pressure I felt. That's why I was trying so hard to force myself to be someone I wasn't.

The message of authenticity saved me from a lifetime of pretending to be an extrovert. I accepted who I am and how my brain responds to stimulants. I'm an introvert, and that's OK. That doesn't mean I'm going to lock myself away in a cabin in the woods, surround myself with books, and never go out in public again. No. But when I have a long night full of social interactions, I know I need to give myself some quiet time alone before going back out in the world. If I don't, I'll be miserable.

Here's another area where I've embraced authenticity: I've been single most of my 20s. Outside the church that's not out of the ordinary. The rest of the world is full of people waiting until their mid-30s to get married. In the church? PEOPLE ARE STARTING TO WORRY ABOUT ME

A lot of my friends are either already married or about to be. It's so annoying because they all say the same thing: "When you find the right person you *just know*." That doesn't make any sense to me at all. There's nothing in my life that I "just know." I can't even "just know" if it's *just* going to be a fart or not.

My main priority in my 20s was ministry. I felt called to travel and speak, and that took up most of my focus. I even bought a minivan, took out the back seats, put a bed in there, and lived in it for two and a half years as I performed around the country. You know how hard it is to get a date while living in a van? When I picked a girl up, I'd have to explain why there was a bed in the back. "I promise I'm not a creep. I live in here. Please don't run away!"

In the church (at least in the circles I found myself in) there is an unspoken timeline everyone is supposed to follow. You go to college, get married, start a career, have a kid, and then have at least one more. The way people were talking to me made me feel like I had missed the deadline for marriage. I was behind, and I needed to catch up, or else everyone would think there's something wrong with me. What if I had let that pressure win me over? "I just need to hurry up and get married" is a terrible way to propose to your girlfriend. I could have rushed into a relationship without thinking just to please some judgmental eyes watching from afar.

The message of authenticity told me not to worry. Everyone is different. You don't have to do what everyone else is doing. There is no universal timeline. You're allowed to have your own priorities. You do you. I owe a lot to my culture's emphasis on authenticity.

I wanted to make that clear before I say anything critical about it. I don't want to start this book off sounding like a grumpy jerk shouting *You fools need to stop listening to Diet Coke commercials! Stop being yourself!* The first time a friend of mine made a comment against authenticity, I got really defensive. I was closed off to any discussion because I knew it changed my life and saved me from a lot of heartaches.

If we want to see the flaws in our world's love of authenticity, we should start by looking at why the message is even appealing in the first place.

Why do we like the idea of finding all meaning, purpose, truth, and identity inside ourselves?

If you think about it, it fits perfectly in with American culture's love of independence. Authenticity can mean you are 100% self-sustained. You don't need anyone or anything to find life's answers. It's all in you. You've got it. America loves that.

American culture idolizes independence. The American dream is all about pulling yourself up by your bootstraps and making success happen by yourself. No handouts. No help. You can make something of yourself just by working hard and never giving up. That's the only respectable way to do it.

You can tell how much we love independence by how much we hate dependence. We only use that term in negative contexts. We say someone has a drug dependency because they're an addict. One of the greatest failures our American imagination can think of is someone in their 30s, living in their parents' basement, still depending on them for financial support. *Why can't you just do it on your own? Why are you using other people? Get your life together, and stop being a burden on others.*

What should we do with the fact that Christianity never treats independence as a virtue?

God calls us to be dependent on Him and the church. In fact, you could argue that to be independent is to be in sin, separated from His will.

People love to talk about how Christianity is not a religion, it's a relationship. You need to have a personal relationship with Jesus. Right. Yeah. Great. That's true, but we need to talk more about what type of relationship it is. There are all different types. Your relationship with your parents is different from your relationship with your friend, which is different from the relationship you have with the server at your favorite restaurant. Jesus isn't looking for any type of relationship you're willing to have with Him. He has a specific one in mind.

Jesus desires to be the Lord of your life. The boss. The one in charge. The one calling the shots.

If I'm going to be honest, to my American, independence loving ears, that actually sounds embarrassing. *I am going to have someone else tell me what to do my whole life? I don't want that! That makes me look pathetic. What's wrong with me that I can't figure it out on my own? Why do I need someone else?*

The main reason I want to reject the idea of trusting someone else more than I trust myself is because I don't believe anyone else is trustworthy.

In every movie about people becoming their authentic self, there's always some clueless, oppressive authority figure trying to force the hero to be someone they're not. They're the villain. You feel for the hero because this antagonist has no idea what they're talking about. It's like they don't even see who this person really is. If the hero conformed, they would be miserable for the rest of their life. I get why stories like that exist. There are a lot of unqualified people trying to tell others what to do.

During seasons of depression, I had people trying to "fix me" by telling me, *Just get over it. You've got nothing to be sad about. Suck it up and get on with your life.* I don't want anyone like that to be the Lord of my life. I don't want someone who doesn't understand introverts always demanding I act like an extrovert. Some people don't like that I make jokes when I preach. They think I'm too silly and immature. If they were in charge, I'd finally "grow up" and stop doing comedy in ministry. I would not trust any one of these people with my life because they're not trustworthy.

But then again, am *I*? What makes me think I can trust myself? If I look inside myself to find who I really am, I'm going to see some wild stuff. There will be some good, but also some evil and selfish parts We all have conflicting desires.

I want to work hard, I also want to sleep all day.

I would love to have abs, I also love eating a whole pizza by myself.

I want to steal little things from grocery stores just to see if I can get away with it.

I want to be a supportive friend, I also feel better about myself when I'm judgmental and looking down on the dumb decisions my friends make.

How do we figure out which impulses to follow?

Which ones are the "real me?" More importantly, is the "real me" someone I should even aspire to be?

That guy could turn out to be a real jerk who makes me miserable.

If you only listen to your heart, you'd be a mess, being tossed by the ever-changing waves of your conflicting desires.

Handing over control and making Jesus the Lord of your life doesn't have to feel like a sacrifice. It's not that you're giving up your freedom and independence just because that's the awful price you have to pay if you want to get into heaven. The fact that Jesus is willing to be your Lord is a gift. It's a blessing.

I am not smart enough to be the Lord of my life. The book of Proverbs says I'm supposed to trust the Lord and not lean on my own understanding. That makes total sense because I have no idea what I'm doing on my own.

When I am in charge of my life, I am the one who tells me how to treat others and how to treat myself. I am responsible for deciding how I'll deal with my depression. What do I know?! Why should I be trusted with that kind of responsibility? All I can see is what's right in front of me. All I have is my own thoughts and feelings rattling around in my brain. That's not enough for me to always know how to move around in this world.

Imagine a flute player in a marching band. I picked flute because that's what I played in 5th grade. I chose it because that's what the girl I had a crush on played and it meant I got to sit next to her.

This flute player is standing in his opening position on the field. What if when the song starts, he says to himself, "You know what? I'm going to do whatever I feel like. I'm going to walk to the right for a while. I'll go backward now. Then I'll just spin around until the song is over." If he does that he's going to make a huge mess. Someone is going to get hurt. Instruments are going to be broken. Someone might end up choking on a tuba.

The flute player has to trust the conductor up in the stands. He's looking down on all of the moving parts. He knows how everything needs to move and fit together. The only thing the flute player can see is what's right in front of him. He needs to entirely rely on the conductor because of his perspective. He's the one with the vision of how the flute player needs to move so he'll fit into this big beautiful picture.

It might feel uncomfortable for the flute player to make a move where he steps backward and to the right, but he knows it's the right move for that moment. Even though there was just a trombone player standing in the very spot the flute player is now heading to, he knows the conductor is moving all things for the good of the whole band.

No one thinks less of the flute player for being completely dependent on the conductor. He can't make it through the movements on his own. He needs the conductor.

It's not like the flute player will ever outgrow his need for the conductor. He won't mature to a point where he can figure out every move on his own. There's always going to be a new song to learn. A musician who has been performing for years isn't ridiculed for needing guidance and correction while learning a new piece. The relationship between the flute player and the conductor is never supposed to change. He can always trust the conductor.

This is the relationship God wants to have with us.

The beautiful part of this relationship is that the conductor doesn't sit silently in the stands expecting us to figure out how we should act and where we should step all on our own. Not only does He give instructions (commandments) but He also sends His son down on the field to join the band. This is a huge deal. The conductor's son humbles himself, puts on the ridiculous uniform, steps on to the field, handling his performance perfectly. He nails every step, every move, asking us to follow His lead. Any time someone in the band feels lost, they can look to the conductor's son's performance to see how it's done.

Jesus lived a perfect life. He loved God and people perfectly. In his ministry, Jesus always told his followers, *Do this because I'm doing this.* He lived as an example of the perfect human. When I make Him the Lord of my life, I follow His lead.

This is where the metaphor falls apart.

I've never seen a marching band where one player gives the perfect performance, then lets himself get killed so the rest of the marching band can have a relationship with the conductor. That would be a very traumatic halftime show. But that's what Jesus did.

In His death, He made a way where there was no way.

In His life, He showed us the way to follow Him.

The same Spirit that was with Jesus is now with us, guiding us, calling us out, and making us more like Him.

The very nature of this relationship means that I am vulnerable. I'm not holding back, only trusting Jesus when I hit rock bottom. It's my everyday life. If I'm leaning on Him, putting the full weight of my trust on Jesus, I'm so vulnerable! If He's not trustworthy, I will fall on my face.

If your main priority is authenticity, there's no point in ever being vulnerable. You believe everything you need is inside you. You don't have to open up, show weakness, ask for help, or trust others. It's on you. You've got it.

Do you see the great relief of taking that responsibility off yourself? With a new and trustworthy Lord, I am not doomed to live at the mercy of my conflicting desires. Following Jesus means I can hold up His life as a filter, to organize what I find when I look inside myself.

When there's part of me that wants to hold a grudge against someone who has wronged me, but there's part of me that wants to forgive so I can have my friend back, Jesus points the way. When I desire to say the meanest sarcastic comment after someone is rude to me, but I also want to be kind and loving to everyone I meet, Jesus can point the way.

Following the way of Jesus is to walk in his footsteps and live your life following his example. This means I'm more concerned about being like Jesus than I am about being myself. But that doesn't mean I'm erasing myself entirely.

Aimee Mann is a singer-songwriter and co-host of the podcast *The Art of Process*. In the first episode, she describes a Q&A session at a poetry conference where high school students could hear from professional poets. A student asked how they could find their voice as a writer. One poet's advice was to not worry so much about that at first. Your main priority should be mastering the rules and structure of poetry. Just focus on that. As you get more comfortable writing within the form, your voice and style will start to take shape on its own. You'll experiment and discover how you personally express yourself best within a poem. This is how I understand how a Christian should respond to a world obsessed with authenticity.

Our top priority shouldn't be finding our voice—our authentic self—but in becoming like Jesus. As we grow and mature in our pursuit of living like Jesus, we'll discover how that looks specifically in our lives. The message of authenticity still has a place in Christianity, but it doesn't reign supreme.

Often scripture tells us *what* to do, but it's our relationship with the Holy Spirit that tells us *how*. We read that we're to go and make disciples, but that's going to look different for everyone in the church. A seventh-grade boy and an eighty-year-old grandma won't share the gospel in the same way. At least, I hope not. If they did, that would either be a weird seventh-grade boy or a super cool grandma.

Even the apostle Paul writes about how each is given gifts and roles within the body of Christ. They're all different. They're all important.

Paul's encouragement was probably in response to people feeling down about how they fit into the ministry of the church. They needed to hear that it's OK to be yourself as you live out Jesus in the world. But we always have to make sure we keep our priorities straight.

What is more important: following Jesus or being yourself? When you go soul searching, a lot of the conflicting desires you'll find sound nothing like Jesus. They might be the exact opposite of what Jesus would do. Are we sometimes throwing out aspects of who He is because they don't fit with who we think we are? Some of us are bad at making friends and would rather not put ourselves out there and let people get close to us. Does that mean we don't have to join the community of the church? Some of us are very shy and introverted, but does that mean we don't have to make disciples? No. Of course not. We just have to find our voice within the structure.

When we live with our priorities out of order, being authentic over being like Jesus, authenticity can become a shield against any need for change.

Most of the time we're not doing this consciously. I can't imagine someone is reading the Bible and when it says something uncomfortable (like forgive those who have hurt you, pray for your enemies, fight against your sin), they shout, *Yeah right! I'm not doing that.* It's a more subtle compromise you might not even notice.

Authenticity can be used as a good excuse to compromise. We see where Jesus is leading us, but we don't believe we're capable of following. We'd never say it out loud, but we think, *Jesus says to love even those who hate you, but I know myself too well. I'm really good at holding a grudge. There's no way I can follow in Jesus' footsteps because that's not who I am.*

Much of the language used to describe a Christian life has to do with movement. You walk in the Spirit. You run the race. You follow Jesus. You go and make disciples. On the other hand, the language of authenticity is about standing in your truth. Plant your feet. Dig in your heels. This is who you are. If that message goes unchecked, if it's the only comfort we give to people, it's as if we're dooming them to be exactly who they are forever. There's no hope for change or growth. What you've got is what you've got. The end. Goodbye.

Authenticity stops feeling like freedom.Instead, it feels like an anchor, weighing you down, holding you back from changing.

When you'r e the Lord of your life, you're not free, you're trapped. Doomed to be a slave to whatever conflicting desires you find within yourself.

But there is a conductor who knows exactly how you fit into the big, beautiful picture He is designing in the world.

You have a spot in the band that is unique to you.

The only way to join in on the song is to make yourself vulnerable and trust Him.

But don't worry, He is trustworthy.

We can trust Him to search our hearts and minds and lead us into what is right.

It's just like the ending of Psalm 139:

> Search me, O God, and know my heart!
> Try me and know my thoughts!
> And see if there be any grievous way in me,
> and lead me in the way everlasting!
> (Psalm 139:23-24)

Are you ready to pray that prayer? Are you ready to join the band? Do you see the joy and relief that comes from leaning on God? You don't have to pretend to have it all figured out. He's got you.

## REFLECTION QUESTIONS

Where do you see the message of authenticity in the culture around you?

Has it been helpful for you personally? If so, how?

What is one way you'd like to be more like Jesus, but you're not sure if you can?

CHAPTER 2

# SOMETHING GOOD IS COMING

*[On Hope]*

"A thrill of hope the weary world rejoices
For yonder breaks a new and glorious morn"

*O Holy Night*

T here's an interview with musician Andrew Peterson where he describes a season of severe depression in his life. When things were at their darkest, the weight of his feelings unbearable, his wife would wrap her arms around him and whisper, "Something good is coming."[1] She'd repeat it over and over as a way to comfort him. "Something good is coming. Something good is coming." It's the perfect message of hope. When you're at your lowest, it's hard to imagine yourself ever not feeling the way you do at that moment. You wholeheartedly believe this is going to last forever. You'll never escape.

When Peterson was at that point, his wife reminded him things would change. Even if he couldn't believe it at that moment, she was there to believe it for him. Something good was coming. That's a beautiful definition of hope: the certainty that change is on its way.

In my darkest moments with my depression, I believed I was hopeless, change was impossible. I was going to feel what I was feeling every day for the rest of my life. It was miserable. *Why even go on? If this is what my life will always be, why not just give up?*

Have you felt that way? Not just with depression or mental health, but in any aspect of life? There was something in your life that you had given up hope could ever change. Your family, your relationships, your addiction, your insecurities, your anger, your faith—maybe your future. Not only did you think nothing good as coming, you were also confident that nothing good was even possible.

It's like the story of the frog and the scorpion. A frog was getting ready to cross the river when a scorpion approached, asking for a ride across the water on the frog's back.

"No way," said the frog, "You're a scorpion. You'll sting me. I'll die."

The scorpion replied, "Why would I do that? I'll be on your back. I can't swim. If I sting you, I'll die too." The scorpion had a point.

The frog was convinced, letting the scorpion climb on his back, he began to swim across the river. Halfway to the other side, the frog felt a sting on his head. The scorpion had stung him.

"Why did you do that?" the frog asked as the poison took hold.

"I'm a scorpion. It's what I do."

The scorpion was doomed because he had no hope that change was possible. This is just how he is. This is what he does. And it killed him.

How many addicts feel like that scorpion? How many people struggling with their relationships? There are probably a ton of people dealing with lust, anger, jealousy, and countless other sins that have totally given up, simply saying, "I guess I'm a scorpion and this is just what I do." There's no hope, only despair. They believe nothing good is coming. Nothing will ever change. They think they're stuck feeling that way, living out the same mistakes for the rest of their lives.

If there's no hope, there's no reason to ever let yourself be vulnerable. The whole motivation behind letting your guard down, opening up, and being in the altogether is that you want things to change. You're willing to take that first step and talk about what's going on because you believe that once you do something good is coming. Without hope, what's the point? Why bring it up? You'll just be rocking the boat. You don't want to bother anyone with your problems. You might as well keep them to yourself.

For the longest time, I couldn't see any reason to tell someone about my depression. I was convinced nothing could possibly change, so what good would it do talking about it? It would just bum people out and ruin the mood if I brought it up. People wouldn't look at me the same way again. I'd be labeled "depression guy" in everyone's mind. They'd want to try to fix me, but I was sure they couldn't, so all their bad advice would do more harm than good.

So what changed?

What made me finally tell someone?

Hope.

It wasn't until I believe something good was possible that I finally spoke up.

Making yourself vulnerable always feels risky. It's a brave step to take with someone, requiring a great deal of courage. Hope is what makes that courage come alive. Hope tells you that you can do it. It's worth it. Something good is on the other side. Go for it.

Look at the stories in the New Testament of those who saw hope in Jesus, and you'll see unstoppable courage.

There was the woman who had been struggling with continuous bleeding for twelve years. Luke writes that she had spent all her money on doctors, but none of them could heal her. When Jesus was passing through her town, there was a great crowd surrounding him. This woman believed Jesus was her hope; with Him things could actually change. Hope turned to courage, and she fought through this giant crowd just so she could touch His clothes. She knew this man had power, and merely touching Him could heal her. She was right. Immediately, she felt herself healed. For twelve years she was told by doctors that this is what the rest of her life would look like. Without hope, she would have never left her house the day Jesus was in town. Without hope, there would have been no reason to fight through the crowd.

There was the time some men believed Jesus could heal their paralyzed friend, so they carried him on his bed all the way to where Jesus was teaching. They couldn't get through the giant crowd, so they went up on the roof, lowering their friend through the tiles in the ceiling before Jesus. They wouldn't have done any of that without hope.

Why bother reaching out if there was no hope? Why seek help? Why leave your comfort zone?

Can I tell you an embarrassing story? I didn't know I was lactose intolerant until I was in college. Now, I don't mean I didn't become lactose intolerant until college. No. I always had been but was totally oblivious. I didn't realize something was wrong until I had a conversation with my mom, where I found myself saying, "What do you mean you're not supposed to have diarrhea every day?" I thought I was healthy! I never spoke up or went to the doctor because I thought this was just how things were always going to be. When the hope that my situation could improve came to me, I was willing to step out and make an appointment. I was even willing to get a colonoscopy. That's how powerful hope is.

Do you believe things can change?

Here's an even tougher question: do you believe *people* can change?

I know many would answer with a loud and confident no. They are sold on the idea that people cannot change.

We see this in how we treat people on the Internet. Whenever you see a celebrity's name trending on Twitter, they've either died or they're being "canceled," meaning they've said or done something inappropriate and the public has decided they are now done with this person. Sometimes it can be a pretty big scandal that not only gets them canceled but also jail time. But there are other cases where the reaction is just as extreme even when the celebrity just made a bad joke they didn't realize was offensive. They still get canceled. The idea is that they have shown their true self and now we shouldn't want anything to do with them. It's not wrong to speak out against a public figure, but I do find it interesting that we've gotten to a point where cancellation is always the first response. Immediate cancellation. There's no mass call for the celebrity to apologize. There's zero expectation that they're even capable of changing. This is who they are. This is who they will always be, so just get rid of them.

Do you believe you can change?

All of Christianity is built on the hope of change. That's what the gospel is all about.

My favorite movie of all time is Tim Burton's *Big Fish*. I know it's not the best movie ever made, but personally, it means a lot. One of the best sections of the film starts with the hero, Edward Bloom, visiting a circus. At the end of the performance, the crowd gets up to leave. From across the tent, Edward sees the most beautiful girl he's ever laid eyes on. It's love at first sight. At that moment he knows this is the girl he'll marry. Now all he has to do is go over and meet her. But the crowd is too big, and he can't fight his way through in time. She's left. Edward is devastated. He's missed his chance to meet the girl of his dreams. But all hope is not lost.

When Edward ends up talking to the ringleader of the circus, he mentions this mystery girl. The ringleader realizes he knows her. He's a friend of her family. Edward begs the ringleader to tell him who she is, but he refuses, "Forget it, kid. She's out of your league." Edward can't give up, so he strikes a deal. Edward is willing to work at the circus, doing any odd job they need, and as payment, every month the ringleader must tell him something new about this girl, the love of his life.

The first month Edward is hard at work, doing anything and everything they ask. As promised, at the end of the month, the ringleader appears, "She likes music." To me, that sounds like kind of a cheat. That doesn't really tell you anything new about this girl. Everyone likes music. Pretty obvious. He didn't even specify what type of music. For Edward, it's enough to keep him going. It's all he can think about as he works dangerous and dirty jobs around the circus.

Another month passes and the ringleader comes to him, "She's going to college." Again, it's all Edward needs to keep going. "College, she's going to college," he repeats to himself over and over. He's in love. Another month: "Her favorite flower is daffodil."

On he goes shoveling elephant poop, getting shot out of cannons, and taming lions. It's all worth it just to learn about this girl he loves. Eventually, the ringleader agreed to tell Edward the name of this girl and where he could finally meet her. This was the moment he was waiting for. He would see her face to face.

Every Christmas, I think about that part of the movie because it reminds me of the Israelites' experience all throughout the Old Testament. God promises them a hero, a savior who would show up and change everything. The Israelites knew they needed this. They recognized that things were not right in the world.

In the beginning, the first humans had the perfect relationship with God, but when they rebelled, becoming the lords of their own lives, they separated themselves from Him. God's perfect design for the world was broken. There was now death and suffering.

It wasn't supposed to be this way.

Israel needed this hero who could bring change.

They had no idea who he would be or when he'd show up. You read their story in the Old Testament and see them get tired of waiting and turn to other gods as a new hope. *If the God of Abraham won't save us, maybe this statue will.* Over and over God restores hope in His chosen people, not only by reminding them that He will never give up on His promise (no matter how many times they reject Him, only to return later) but by offering new information about this coming savior.

A prophet would show up with a message from God. One would say, "He will come from the town of Bethlehem." I picture Israel reacting like Edward, this being enough to bring them back to hold out hope for the savior.

Over time they learn more.

"He will die for the sins of the world."

"He will be bruised and beaten so you can be healed."

"He will teach in parables."

Israel didn't just repeat these promises to themselves as they worked through their day. They wrote them down, and we have them all throughout the Old Testament. They were the reminders they needed that God would fulfill His promise.

These prophecies were God's way of saying, "Something good is coming."

Then one silent night, as shepherds watched their sheep, angels appeared before them to say, "He's here. The one you've been waiting for is here. Come and see him."

O Holy Night is my favorite Christmas song, mostly for one specific line: "A thrill of hope, the weary world rejoices." A thrill of hope. Hope is thrilling. It's beyond exciting to believe, to know that this too shall pass. This will change! It will lift. The old will go away, and something new and greater will take its place.

Jesus is our source of hope. He came down to earth and became the first and only human to live a perfect life. He was the only one who deserved Heaven. He earned it. He deserved an intimate relationship with God, deserved to have His prayers heard.

The rest of us have separated ourselves from God by becoming the lords of our own lives. We tricked ourselves into thinking we were trustworthy enough to be in charge, even though we had no idea what we were doing. Any human who tries to be their own lord is going to cause damage to God's perfect order. The price for that is death. Justice is essential to God; there must be punishment. That's what we deserve. There's nothing we could ever do to change that on our own. We are doomed.

But Jesus did not come to live a perfect life for His own sake. He did it on our behalf because He knew we never could. He came to switch places with us. He came to take on all we deserve so He could give us what He deserves. He died, suffering on the cross. That was supposed to be our death. That was supposed to be me up there. That's the consequences for my life. He took it away from me and gave me instead of the gift of what He deserved. That changes everything.

I've had the chance to witness the birth of hope in the lives of people who never thought it was possible.

One of my most memorable encounters came at the end of a youth service when a high school girl approached me during the response time. I don't know how else to describe her, except that she just looked normal. I know that sounds dumb. She looked like the most normal high school girl ever. I didn't know what she could have possibly needed prayer for until she started to tell me about her home life. Her mom was a fitness instructor but also an alcoholic. Every night when she came home, she'd begin to drink. The more she drank, the more she said things you should never say to your children. She'd look at her daughter across the dinner table and say things like, "Look at how disgusting you are. You're so out of shape. It's pathetic. I could outrun you and I'm twice your age." Night after night she'd go off until eventually, her daughter started believing it. She told me she began planning her meals by what would be the easiest to throw up. Her mother had convinced her that she was repulsive and unlovable the way she was.

Next thing I know, she's crying because she's never admitted to any of this out loud. I'm trying not to cry myself because I can tell how hurt she is.

I thanked her for trusting me enough to open up.

"But here's the problem," I said. "After this service, I leave and travel to wherever I'm speaking next. It would be really great if you had someone here with you who you could talk to about this. Is there any leader here that we could go talk to together about this?" She said she'd be willing to tell her youth pastor. We found where he was and waved him over. I could tell she was still a little nervous so I led,

"Hey man, we were just talking, and she's going through something right now that she wanted to talk to you about."

As she began to tell him the story, I slowly backed away and watched from afar. It was so beautiful to see. I was witnessing her being introduced to the hope of change that is available because of Christ.

Hope for a new identity not wrapped up in what others think about her but in who Jesus is.

A new way of looking at herself loved and approved because of Jesus' death for her.

A new family full of new adults who will speak life and encouragement. They will point her to Jesus and show her the same love that He has for her.

A new God who loves her just the way she is.

A new lord of her life who will lead her when she feels lost.

A new savior whose sacrifice covers any imperfection she's afraid of showing.

Something good had arrived in her life and it was thrilling to watch.

Have you given up hope? Is there anything in your life you've just accepted will always be broken? It doesn't have to be this way. Change is possible. Renew your hope. Let it turn to courage. Not only is something good coming, He's here. He's done the work we can't so we can have the incredible change we don't deserve.

He's here.

## REFLECTION QUESTIONS

What is one positive change Christ and the church has brought to your life?

Describe a season or situation where you needed to hear that "something good is coming."

Do you ever feel like hope is embarrassing? We live in a cynical world and sometimes it can feel ridiculous to hope that things can change. Do you agree? Why or why not?

# CHAPTER 3

# WHERE YOU ARE

*[The Role of Vulnerability]*

"The secret of life is honesty and fair dealing. If you can fake that, you've got it made."

Groucho Marx

You can't fix a problem unless you're willing to admit the problem exists.

Imagine you're at a car mechanic waiting for them to finish your oil change when this old, ugly, busted up car pulls in. There's smoke coming from the engine, one of the tires is flat, and it's making a million horrible noises. The manager goes out to talk to the driver.

"What can we do for you?"

"Nah. I'm good."

"Excuse me?"

"Yeah. Everything is great."

"There's nothing wrong?"

"Nope."

"Sir, your car sounds like it has asthma."

"How dare you!"

The car won't get the help and attention it needs until the owner is willing to say, "I think something is wrong."

If you go to the doctor for a check-up and never mention the pain you're feeling, you won't get help. Your stomach feels like it's on fire, your knees are made of jello, and you cry blood, but if you don't say anything about it, you won't get treated.

I realize this is easier said than done.

Have you ever had something in your life you felt like you couldn't say out loud? I call these Black Hole topics. They're the topics that feel too big and too scary to let out. If we ever brought it out of hiding, it would be a disaster. It would be like bringing out a black hole, destroying everything. It would ruin the mood of whatever conversation you're having. It would change the way people look at you. You'd lose friends. Everything would get pulled inside it. It's too powerful to let out so you might as well do your best to keep it locked away. It might be an addiction, wounds from something in your past, fears, doubts, or struggles with mental health. I wish I could write out a definitive list of what these topics are, but they're different for everyone, and each one is significant when you are the one experiencing it. Some kids have no problems talking about their parents' divorce, while others are mortified by the thought of bringing it up. There are communities where it's acceptable to talk honestly about mental health while there are those that aren't.

Have you ever felt that way about something in your life?

A broken relationship?

A sin?

A repeated behavior that was pushing people away?

You knew it was there. You knew it was a problem. You were afraid that talking about the black hole would only make things worse. You convinced yourself that you'd be able to handle what you were going through entirely on your own. Even though your way of dealing with it was to not deal with it. It's like your bedroom is on fire and your solution is just to get up and move to the living room so you can keep watching TV. You might be in the clear for now, but the house is still on fire.

After a while, I just get used to the Black Holes being there. I give up on the hope of things changing because it's been a part of my life for so long. I just hide it, telling myself it can't affect me when it's buried away.

Edgar Allen Poe's *A Telltale Heart* is about a killer who thinks he's gotten away with the perfect murder after he hides the dead body under the floorboards of his home. When the police make an unexpected visit, he begins to lose his mind. He's trying to keep his cool and focus on acting casual, but he swears he can hear the beating of the dead man's heart from under the floor. It's so loud! He thinks he's been caught. There's no way the police can't hear it too. Finally, the killer breaks down. He can't take it anymore. Even though the body was buried, it still haunted him.

I've heard the heartbeat under the floorboards. When I feel like I've done my best to hide away the black holes in my life, I'm still on edge, never fully present, because I'm haunted by the weight I'm carrying. It never ends well. I grew up in church, but I was still too scared to tell anyone about my depression or suicidal thoughts. I kept them to myself and it was killing me inside. There was part of me that never wanted to let the secret out but another part that wished I would.

In *A TellTale Heart*, the killer knew that once what was buried away was discovered his life was over. That's the same fear we often have even though the exact opposite is true.

There's something about admitting the problem exists that changes our perspective.

Mister Rogers said,

> Anything that's human is mentionable, and anything that is mentionable can be more manageable. When we can talk about our feelings, they become less overwhelming, less upsetting, and less scary. The people we trust with that important talk can help us know that we are not alone.[1]

If you can take the wildly brave first step of talking about what's going on, you can begin to deal with it.

There's a phrase in 12 Step programs: "You're only as sick as your secrets."[2] It's the inverse of what Mister Rogers is saying: anything we feel like we CAN'T mention CAN'T be more manageable. Anything we deem unspeakable must be too big, too terrifying, too impossible to handle. It's like a monster lurking in the shadows. You know it's there, but as long as it's in the dark, you have no idea what it looks like. Your imagination can run wild, picturing it as huge and dangerous. But when we can talk about it, it's like shining a spotlight into the darkness. Sure, you can see the monster really does exist, but now that you've got a good look at it, maybe you're not as scared. With some help, you can take this thing on.

Maybe for you, it's not some enormous horrible darkness looming over your life. It's not how big the problem is that makes you want to keep it to yourself, but how small it is.

*I'm struggling with jealousy* can sound ridiculous to say out loud. It feels like such a minor issue, you should be able to get over it. Or maybe you find yourself feeling down for no reason. It's not quite sadness because there's nothing to feel sad about. Everything is fine. Yet some days you can't get out of bed. You've heard other people talk about their struggles with depression, but you don't think that could be you. *What do I have to be depressed about?*

It can be anything, big or small. You feel like an idiot because you think you of all people shouldn't be dealing with that. You can't imagine telling anyone. Everyone thinks you've got it all together. You can't let them down. *What will they think when they find out what a mess I am?*

Why do we do this? Why do we punish ourselves for where we are? We tell ourselves *I shouldn't feel this way* or *I shouldn't be struggling with this anymore.* But you are! That's where you are right now, so who cares if you should or not? You don't get free by ignoring it.

Imagine you're driving to a friend's house and you get lost. They just moved into a new neighborhood that isn't registered on your GPS, so you have to call them to get directions. The first question they're going to ask is where you are. You don't want to answer because you are SUPER lost. You're on the complete opposite side of town. It's baffling how you got this turned around. You're really embarrassed, so when they ask, you lie about where you are. Now, none of the help they offer will do you any good. The directions won't make sense unless they know exactly where you are. *I shouldn't be this lost,* you think. That's ok. Right now "should" doesn't matter. What's important is where you actually are.

Being emotionally and spiritually in the altogether opens the door to change. When we let our walls down and admit we're not perfect, we can deal with what's wrong.

I want to pause for a moment on admitting we're not perfect. That's something we're really good at in the abstract, but it's a lot more uncomfortable when we have to get into the details. In vague terms, it's safe and easy: *Oh yeah. I'm totally messed up. I need God because I'm broken and wicked. I'm terrible on my own.* But what if you are asked to get specific? What's in your life right now that's broken and wicked? Not just in general terms. Be real. What's not perfect in your life today? Where are you at right now in your relationship with Christ?

That feels so much scarier.

And it should!

Vulnerability is risky.

Think of how we use the term in contexts besides relationships. When you are vulnerable, you're open to attack, your weakness is exposed, and you could be utterly destroyed. It's dangerous to have a vulnerability in your armor, your defenses, or your strategy. The same is true with social vulnerability. The armor comes off when you open up to someone. You have no idea how they'll respond. Hopefully, you've chosen someone you trust, but there's still a level of uncertainty. They could use this to destroy you. They could hold it over your head. They might not ever look at you the same way again. Being vulnerable means opening yourself up for the possibility of being hurt.

How scary is that? But with the right people on the other side of your vulnerable moment, you'll be taking the first steps towards change. We need that first moment. We can't bring change on our own.

Remember, God designed us to be dependent.

Our dependence is not just on our God, but on his church, too. There are a lot of metaphors the Bible gives to help us understand the church: it's the bride of Christ, a family, and a body. All of these bring about images of connection, belonging, and dependence. This is totally on purpose.

We see times where the church is called to take care of each other financially. Do you shudder at the idea of needing the church to help pay your bills because you've fallen on hard times? That's a stab right in the pride to think you've got to rely on others. Maybe that's the point. Our obedience will kill our pride so we can participate freely in the body of Christ.

My pastor uses the image of the church as a body to illustrate our dependence on each other.[3] The apostle Paul says we are many parts that make up the body of Christ. A body part can only function when it's connected to the whole. It also can't heal unless it's attached to the rest of the body. If you stab a finger that's already been cut off, that wound will never be able to heal. In the same way that the body can send signals and supplies to your wounded finger to close the wound and heal, the body of Christ is there to provide the support in your time of need. Paul says that we are to bear each other's burdens. This acknowledges that there are hurts too heavy for us to carry on our own.

Don't think you're miraculously the only Christian on the planet who doesn't need to lean on God and the church.

Even Jesus models vulnerability in the garden the night before he's arrested. In Matthew 26, we read that Jesus confides in his closest disciples about how he's feeling about his coming death. He asks them to stay up and pray with him, then he goes off alone to take his feelings to God. If even Jesus finds himself in moments where he needs to be vulnerable with people he trusts, what makes us think we can avoid it?

The majority of churches probably don't disagree with this in theory, but are we actually living this out? When was the last time you found yourself being open and vulnerable with someone in your life?

Is there any area of your life where you find you're really good at dodging opportunities of vulnerability? Anytime you feel it bubbling up to the surface, you can still push it back down and tell yourself there's no need to involve other people. *It's not that big of a deal. It's not worth talking about. People don't need to know this.*

There's a moment in the first *Ant-Man* film that really articulates my own struggle with this. Scott Lang, played by Paul Rudd, crashes his daughter's birthday party, much to her surprise. She loves her dad, and you can tell she's so excited to see him. Her mom, Scott's ex, is not so thrilled. He's not allowed to show up unannounced. He just got out of prison and he hasn't paid any of the child support he owes. His ex says he needs to get his act together, then he can spend time with his daughter. Scott's ex says, "Be the man she already thinks you are."

When I get trapped in the mindset that I have to have it all together; I feel like I'm trying to become the man I've already tricked people into thinking I am. I'm working just as hard at keeping up appearances as I am trying to deal with my actual issues. But I can only deal with them behind closed doors, and I can't get any real progress because I'm also wrapped up in faking my perfection. That's a lot of work, too.

It's important to remember that there's not a clear cut list of subjects that everyone is always uncomfortable talking about. Some people are ok with opening up about their love lives while others get really nervous. Some are willing to totally own mistakes from their past, others try to pretend they never happened. Some people have no fear at all talking about financial troubles while others, LIKE ME, chicken out.

I'm terrible with money, and I hate talking about it. Dave Ramsey, if you're reading this, get ready to rip someone else's hair out at this story. I'm so sorry.

Ever since I started traveling and speaking full time, I've had to deal with all of the responsibilities that come with being self-employed. I'm my own boss, which is a problem because I'm a terrible boss. A real pushover. It's so easy to convince my boss to let me have the day off for no reason.

I have to be the one who pushes me to work hard. I'm the one in charge of keeping things organized. I have to stay on top of my finances. Or at least try to.

My primary financial strategy is what I like to call "Out of Sight–Out of Mind." Here's what you do: never check your bank account. Ever. Assume you're completely broke and silently freak out every day as you try to spend as little money as possible. At the end of the month, you're allowed to check your account balance once.

Hopefully, the strategy worked, and you'll actually have a lot more money in there than you thought.

Awesome.

Congratulations.

Reward yourself by taking all that extra cash you didn't know you had and spend it recklessly on any dumb thing you want. You'll probably spend too much, and then you'll be too scared to check your bank account to see what you have left. That's perfect. Now you're ready to start the cycle over for the next month.

Is it a perfect system? Of course not. It's so stupid. It rarely works out in my favor. Sometimes you'll check your bank account and realize you weren't worried enough and you have even less money than you thought. In those moments the best thing to do is, take a second, breathe in, and freak out harder than you ever have before because you're in so much trouble!

Having no money is actually a really great motivation to work harder. Sometimes (I'm about to sound like the biggest idiot so get ready, Mr. Ramsey) I'll feel like I need to kick my butt out of being lazy so I'll go buy some big expensive thing I don't really need for the sole purpose of making me a little poorer.

*Let's see you work your way out of this one, Taylor,* I think as I spend $200 on a microphone for my camera that doesn't really sound much better than the $70 microphone I've been using.

I know these are all terrible financial strategies. The main reason I haven't tried anything else is that I know it would require having to ask someone for help. That's so embarrassing. I've been my own boss for almost a decade. You'd think I'd have it figured out by now.

But that's just part of the reason I don't want to reach out to someone. The other part is what REALLY paralyzes me.

If I were to get help, there would come a moment where the other person says, "I'd be glad to help. Tell me about how you've been handling money so far." Then I'd have to look them in the eye and describe what I've just told you. And then I'll have to watch their reaction, whatever that may be. They could laugh in my face. They might yell at me and call me an idiot. They could look down on me for acting like a child and never take me seriously as an adult again. Picturing someone's reaction has always been the main reason I've kept it to myself.

That's also true for my taxes. Being self-employed means, I don't have The Man taking taxes out of every paycheck. Not only do I have to be my own boss but I have to be my own The Man. The last few years I've filed my taxes by myself and...I think I'm doing them, right? I have no idea. I'm winging it. Making it up as I go along with some BOLD guesses on the right way to do it.

My catchphrase as I submit my completed tax form to the government is, "Welp. Let's see if I'm going to jail!"

So far, so good.

Maybe I'm so poor I'm not even on the IRS' radar?

Oh no. I just had a thought.

What if this book becomes a huge hit and I make millions off it? The IRS is going to read this and come after me! I can't have that. I need to make sure this book doesn't become a giant success. I have to do whatever it takes to make sure it isn't a #1 best seller (so if this book comes out and it isn't a smash hit, just know that my plan worked. It was on purpose).

After a while, my tax strategy of "Guess Until You Go to Jail" started affecting me. Whenever tax season would approach, my anxiety would intensify. My mom must have noticed because she recommended I visit a financial advisor who handles taxes for small businesses. I put off setting up an appointment for a long time. Again, I was terrified of what her reaction would be when I told her about my taxes. What if she yelled at me? What if I make her so mad she throws up? Is that possible?

I knew there was some hardcore vulnerability waiting for me at that appointment when I finally called and set it up. It was terrifying. I was already preparing myself for the meeting going badly. I thought if her reaction was too much to handle I'd just immediately leave, never file my taxes again, go off the grid, cut up my social security card, hitchhike to Alaska, and probably die by accidentally eating poison berries.

I'M NOT SUPPOSED TO HAVE WEAKNESSES!

I want to be perfect and have it all figured out! It's so frustrating that I'm not and I don't. I'm far from that. The IRS is going to find out and eat me alive!

When I sat down in the financial advisor's office, about to open up about my problem, I started by letting her know what

I was thinking at that moment.

"I have no idea how big of a mess my taxes are. I'm scared I've been doing them wrong, but I've also dreaded coming to you because I don't want you to get mad at me. Please don't freak out. Please be gentle."

She agreed and braced herself as she asked me questions.

"Did you do your taxes last year?"

"Yes."

"Did you owe money?"

"Yes."

"Did you pay it?"

"Yes."

"Did you do that the year before?"

"Yes."

"OK. Well, you're actually doing way better than a lot of the people who come into my office. I get people haven't paid their taxes in fourteen years, so don't worry."

I was blown away. Fourteen years?! That's wild.

That meeting lifted a few different burdens off of my shoulders. I found out my situation wasn't the worst this lady had ever seen. It was pretty small when you compare it to what it could have been. After that initial relief, she walked me through some simple next steps I needed to take to keep my taxes on track. I thought it was going to be so much more work. Nope, I left with a list of three things I needed to do. That's it.

She helped me shine a light on the monster that was hiding in the corner of my mind. When I got a good look at it for the first time, I realized I could actually take this thing on. That would have never happened if I didn't walk into that vulnerable moment of admitting why I needed help. Up until that meeting, I was desperately trying to become the man people already thought I was. I put on a good face and made everyone think I had it all together. But I was able to find the hope of change when I laid that aside.

When we allow ourselves to be vulnerable, we are saved from having to pretend.

"For to confess is not simply to change but to first face and fully deny the false person you were trying to be," Josh Larsen writes this in his book *Movies Are Prayers*. In his chapter on how movies can be prayers of confession, he looks at Buzz Lightyear's journey in *Toy Story*.

For the majority of the film, Buzz believes he is actually a real-life space ranger, not just a toy. This all comes crumbling down when he happens to see a commercial advertising other Buzz Lightyear toys. Woody tries to cheer up Buzz by saying, "Being a toy is a lot better than being a space ranger.

Larsen says this about that scene:

> Glancing from the corporate stamp on his wrist ("Made in Taiwan") to the hand-lettered inscription on the bottom of his foot ("ANDY"), Buzz comes to understand that his true identity lies not in the facade of a fictitious hero but in being claimed by someone else, someone who loves him despite his faults.[4]

Our God has written His name on your heart. Change comes when you lean on Him. You don't have to pretend to be the hero. You're not perfect. You've admitted it. But now it's OK to dig in and get specific. Even about things that make you uncomfortable.

# REFLECTION QUESTIONS

We read the quote from *Ant-Man* where Scott Lang's ex says "be the man she already thinks you are." Who do you want people to think you are? If you could completely control how people perceive you, what would you want them to see?

Do you agree with Mister Rogers' quote that what is mentionable can be more manageable? If so, how have you seen that be true in your own life?

What Black Hole Topics have you dealt with in your past? What problems felt too big or too scary to say out loud?

# CHAPTER 4

# IN THE ALTOGETHER
# IN THE EVERYDAY

*[5 Vulnerable Moments We All Face]*

"What happens when people open their hearts?"
"They get better."

Haruki Murakami, *Norwegian Wood*

I don't want to let my descriptions of vulnerability stay vague and general.

Let's zoom in and get specific about what it looks like to be in the altogether in the everyday. Here are five situations we all find ourselves in that require us to become vulnerable. If we rise to the occasion, laying down our defenses, there is hope for change.

## BEING WRONG

Top 3 Great Feelings We Don't Talk About Enough
1.  When you go down a hill on a rollercoaster and it feels like your stomach is trying to float away through your throat.
2.  Struggling with a piece of popcorn stuck in your teeth for an hour but finally getting it out.
3.  BEING RIGHT!

Being right feels amazing. You can tell everyone loves it too because most of us are willing to do anything to prove we're right. Have you seen the way people argue on social media?

Those fights are less about convincing the other person and more about showing off how right you are.

If being right is the highest high, then not only realizing you're wrong but also admitting it, is the lowest low. Whether it's finding out something you believed wasn't true (Have you ever realized you were wrong in the middle of an argument but were too embarrassed to admit it? Yeah. Me too.) or thought you were doing the right thing but you discovered later it was all wrong, and your actions might have hurt someone, it never feels good. You're opening yourself up, admitting you're not perfect and exposing yourself to a possible attack on your pride.

Josh Harris is the perfect example of this. In the '90s, when Harris was only twenty-one, he wrote *I Kissed Dating Goodbye*, an incredibly successful book about Christian relationships. It became a number one bestseller, influencing the way youth pastors everywhere talked about dating. Some loved the book while others had a really negative experience with it.

Over the years, people reached out to explain to Harris how his book hurt them, screwed up their view on relationships, or was used as a weapon against them. He listened. Now Harris has a statement on his website about his book and how his opinion on it is changing:

> While I stand by my book's call to sincerely love others, my thinking has changed significantly in the past twenty years. I no longer agree with its central idea that dating should be avoided. I now think dating

can be a healthy part of a person developing rela-
tionally and learning the qualities that matter most in
a partner.[1]

At first, I thought it must have taken a lot of courage to
write something like that. He's announcing to the world that
he no longer believes the very thing that got him famous. Going public with something like that would be terrifying. The
more I looked into Harris' journey, though, the more I started
to think the courage came earlier. By the time he got to the
point where he felt the need to say something publicly, the
momentum from an earlier act of courage was strong enough
to carry him along.

Here's what Harris said in a TEDx Talk called *Strong
Enough to be Wrong*:

> But it was so hard for me to face up to being wrong
> because it felt like I was saying a big part of my life
> was wrong. I didn't have the courage to do that. What
> helped me to begin to let my guard down was a few
> years ago, I stopped being the pastor of a large
> church, and I went back to school. I went to graduate
> school, and I stopped having to be constantly right
> about everything and defend all these ideas, and I
> just became a student who was listening.[2]

For Harris, courage started when he chose to slow down
and listen. Can you imagine what it must have felt like to read

those messages from people explaining how his book hurt them? It would have been so much easier to dismiss them all. That would have been safer. But he was willing to humble himself and examine his beliefs.

In that TEDx Talk, Harris says, "Evolution always involves death." If we want to grow and change, we have to let old habits and ways of thinking die off. You have to make room for the new. That's what change is. We need to create a culture that celebrates the courage it takes to question what in your life needs to change. It has to be a culture that allows the space for people to be open and vulnerable enough to evaluate all the things in their life that may need to die.

But here's where I disagree with Harris. The way he tells it, the big shift that needed to happen was when he stepped away from being a pastor. He says that's when he was able to stop "having to be constantly right about everything." I don't think that mindset is uniquely tied to ministry. I know pastors who don't act that way. A pastor's role isn't necessarily "The One with All the Answers ." Scripture is supposed to stand as the authority, and the pastor is the first follower, helping the congregation see the answers and guidance God's Word gives. A pastor is allowed to be wrong. In fact, it could be a beautiful example for their congregation if a pastor got up and apologized during a service. I also know plenty of people who feel the burden to be right about everything and they are not on staff at a church.

Isn't it crazy that we're all arguing with such extreme conviction on every belief that we have?

Everyone believes they're 100% right about 100% of their beliefs. But that can't possibly be true. Someone has to be wrong.

Why do we always assume it's the other person? There has to be at least *one thing* you're wrong about right now. It could be your priorities in life, how you handle your anger, relationships, biases about other cultures, theology, or a million other things. I'm sure I'm wrong about at least ten things right now. We've got to be willing to slow down and examine.

Growing up in church, I always heard people talk about their doubts surrounding Christianity, and tried my best to ignore them. I was too scared to do any research to find answers for myself. I was afraid of what I might find. What if there really was no proof? What if I realized it didn't make sense and all of Christianity was a lie? It was like I was scared to watch a magic trick too closely because I was afraid I'd figure out how it was done and the illusion would be ruined. This fear kept my faith shallow for a long time. It wasn't until I met people who were more mature in their walk with Christ who encouraged me to question and doubt. It's good to poke and prod at your beliefs. If they topple over after a few questions, they weren't very strong in the first place. It's better to find that out sooner than later. Now you can build up your new beliefs stronger than before.

I have to add one more thought before closing out this section.

About a month before my book came out (the one you're reading right now), Josh Harris made two announcements that shocked a lot of people.

First, he and his wife were divorcing. Second, he no longer considered himself a follower of Christ.

If you're reading this in the immediate aftermath of those announcements in 2019, you could be thinking, *Yikes! Josh Harris is actually the perfect example of why you should never question your beliefs because it can take you to such terrible places.*

If you're reading this in the future, I have no idea what your perspective is. You could be living in the year 3025 and this is the first time you're hearing about Harris. You have more important things to worry about like your alien overlords. Or maybe you're only ten years in the future of when this book was written. Who knows what Harris' life looks like where you are. If he was willing to slow down and evaluate his beliefs once, we can only pray he's willing to do it again.

We all grow. We all change. We go through seasons.

I saw a lot of remarks from Christians online after Harris' announcements that were pretty smug. *Oh, you'll be back!* That's not what I'm saying. I just want to remember that no one's fate is fully revealed to us until death, and even then we might not get the full picture. We might give up on someone's ability to change, but God's view of the situation is always more trustworthy. We shouldn't be afraid to question and to doubt just because of where it led someone else. It's still vital to growth.

Admitting you're wrong will take the courage to make yourself vulnerable but think of the change that will come from it.

Would you rather fight through an uncomfortable moment of being wrong or go your whole life dragging bad beliefs everywhere you go?

## APOLOGIZING

If the thought of having to apologize to someone doesn't make you uncomfortable, you might be doing it wrong. We can learn a lot about how to have an effective apology from a pizza company.

Up until a few years ago, most people thought Domino's pizza was garbage. The company was losing business, closing stores, failing fast. Then the CEO wanted to do something risky. He wanted to admit that their pizza was terrible.

They created an ad campaign that basically said *Hey, we know everyone hates our pizza! We know you think the crust tastes like cardboard! We hear you, and we're fixing it. We're changing how we make pizza because we don't want to suck anymore.*

A lot of people in the company were so nervous about this approach. No one had ever done something like this before. What if it backfired? This could be a disaster.

Not only did the commercial work, it worked better than anyone could have imagined. Two days after the commercial started airing their sales were already growing. By week three, there were stores literally running out of pepperoni. It was a huge hit.

Domino's CEO explained the success this way: "If somebody is going to convince you they're going to change, it has to start with them absolutely owning the problem in the first place."[3] That is the key to a proper apology. Are you really owning it? *I'm sorry I offended you* is such a weak apology. You're pulling back to protect yourself. If you really want to mend a relationship, you have to make yourself vulnerable.

Here's the bummer about apologies: with every other vulnerable moment you get to choose someone you trust to open up to, but you don't get to choose who deserves your apology. It could be someone who hates your guts because of what you did. When you say *I'm sorry* you have no idea how they'll react. They could lord it over you and kick you while you're down. They could twist the knife and enjoy seeing you so humbled. The worst part? You deserve it. You hope they'll show you grace and forgiveness, but you're not guaranteed that. It feels risky to make yourself vulnerable for an effective apology, so a lot of the time we hold back from genuinely owning what we did.

In 2017 the #MeToo movement outed several men in Hollywood for sexual harassment and abuse. Public statements and apologies came rushing out from the accused, but it was clear that, with most of them, their top priority wasn't reconciliation and forgiveness. They just wanted to protect their reputation. They downplayed the severity of their actions or blamed culture for their behavior. Hardly anyone owned what they did wrong.

In January 2018 Dan Harmon, creator of shows like *Community* and *Rick & Morty*, was accused of harassing a writer who worked on one of his shows. Instead of taking the same approach as everyone else in Hollywood, Harmon chose to make himself vulnerable.

In an episode of his podcast, Harmontown, he spent seven minutes OWNING his behavior:

> I lied to myself the entire time about it. And I lost my job. I ruined my show. I betrayed the audience. I destroyed everything, and I damaged her internal compass. And I moved on. I've never done it before, and I will never do it again, but I certainly wouldn't have been able to do it if I had any respect for women. On a fundamental level, I was thinking about them as different creatures. I was thinking about the ones that I liked as having some special role in my life, and I did it all by not thinking about it. So, I just want to say, in addition to obviously being sorry, but that's really not the important thing, I want to say I did it by not thinking about it and I got away with it by not thinking about it. And if she hadn't mentioned something on Twitter, I would have continued to not have to not think about it, although I did walk around with my stomach in knots about it, but I wouldn't have had to talk about it.[4]

Harmon prefaced his statement by saying a lot of people told him he shouldn't even address it. I can see why. He is brutally honest about the wrong he did. It's not a simple, vague, half-hearted apology. It's not a P.R. move to save face. He's actually vulnerable. He's open to attack. This terrible thing he did is now out in the open. It's risky because there's no telling what kind of response this will get.

Shortly after the podcast went live, Megan Ganz, the writer who accused Harmon posted on Twitter:

> Yes I only listened because I expected an apology. But what I didn't expect was the relief I'd feel just hearing him say these things actually happened. I didn't dream it. I'm not crazy. Ironic that the only person who could give me that comfort is the one person I'd never ask. This was never about vengeance; it's about vindication. That's why it didn't feel right to just accept his apology in private (although I did that, too). But if any part of this process should be done in the light, it's the forgiveness part. And so, @danharmon, I forgive you.[5]

Notice where she said the relief came from. It wasn't because he said, "I'm sorry," but from the fact that he owned it.

You have to make yourself vulnerable to give a real apology. Owning the mistake does not feel good. It's a real attack on your pride. But how else will you move forward in your relationship? It's the first step to show that you are willing to change.

The Biblical story of Zacchaeus, the tax collector and wee little man, is the perfect model for how we should apologize.

73

The first thing you need to know about Zacchaeus is that nobody would have liked him. Being a tax collector meant being despised. Rome would hire Jews to collect the taxes on their own people. There was no real oversight so you could easily demand more money than what was owed and keep all the extra profit. They were seen as traitors, joining their oppressors to get rich quick.

When Jesus was passing through town, he singled out Zacchaeus and said they were going to eat together. The people were furious that Jesus would break bread with this wicked man, but Zacchaeus was determined to show everyone that he was willing to change to follow after his new Lord.

"Look, Lord! Here and now I give half of my possessions to the poor, and if I have cheated anybody out of anything, I will pay back four times the amount. (Luke 19:8)"

Think about how uncomfortable it would have been for Zacchaeus as he went from house to house, paying people back. These are people he could have been cheating for years. They answer the door to find Zacchaeus standing there humbled, owning the wrong he did. Yes, it cost him financially, but it also cost him his pride. I can't imagine those conversations were fun or easy for Zacchaeus, but I'm sure they were worth it. The hurt and anger caused by his greed could be replaced with love and community.

Are there people in your life you find yourself avoiding? You know there are still wounds from something you said or did. Think of the broken relationships we've accepted will be broken forever. *This is just how it's going to be forever.* It doesn't have to be. There is hope for change. It often starts with the willingness to make yourself vulnerable and apologize.

## CONFRONTATION

I used to think confrontation meant fighting. It has to be unpleasant. Intense. This person did wrong, and I'm going to give them a piece of my mind! I pull them aside with a Hey, can I talk to you? (the scariest phrase in the English language) and then I let them have it. I talk down to them. I yell. I have all the power. I'm in charge. *You've got to shut up and listen because I've got something to say, punk!*

With that mindset, I was too intimidated to confront anyone. Who am I to attack this person? I'm clearly not doing everything right. I'm screwing up, too. Plus, I don't want to make things uncomfortable. Conflict sucks so I'd rather keep it to myself. Often, though I would end up confronting someone the way I thought I was supposed to, it never went well. The relationship never improved because of the confrontation. Things usually ended up more awkward and tense.

In reality, when you're confronting someone, you're the vulnerable one. You're opening yourself up to tell them how they hurt you. Notice that once again, a vital aspect of vulnerability is humbling yourself. That's never fun. Our love of independence isn't just about being able to succeed without needing anyone, we also like to pretend we can get through life without other people affecting us.

Don't let people see you cry. Don't get offended. Don't care what other people think.

Don't!

Obviously, we can't let everyone in the world get close enough to affect us. People we barely know shouldn't be allowed to get under our skin. Who cares what they think? But the people you love and are close to can say things that hurt. They can act carelessly and make you feel terrible. To confront them means you have to make yourself vulnerable and say, *This is how you've made me feel.*

How will they react? Worst case scenario: they might dismiss you entirely and accuse you of being too sensitive. Best case scenario: they respond with their own vulnerability and apologize. There's no way of knowing unless you take that leap of faith.

Sometimes you have a pretty good idea of how a person will respond. You've seen how they've handled similar confrontations, and it never went well. But you can't just confront the people you know 100% will handle it well. People will always surprise you. We have to give everyone a chance.

Jesus says, "If your brother sins against you, go and tell him his fault, between you and him alone. If he listens to you, you have gained a brother. (Matthew 18:15)" The rest of that passage gives instructions about what to do next if that first confrontation doesn't go well. Even Jesus knows some people are going to be jerks about it. We're still commanded to try and reconcile! We have to make this a part of our everyday lives despite what the outcome may be. We're responsible for the step we can take. What they do with it is not on us.

If they handle it poorly, maybe they're too afraid to be vulnerable and accept that they could be wrong. Just make them read this book first. Duh. Problem solved.

If someone recommended this book to you, they're going to confront you about something. It's just a fact. Prepare yourself. The moment you tell them you finished reading, they're going to sit you down for a terrifying talk. Who knows what it's about? Honestly, that doesn't really matter. What matters is that they're willing to take the brave step of opening up to you about it. Most of us are too scared to do that. We just give up on the relationship altogether, slowly distancing ourselves because we can't handle whatever the problem is and we're too scared to see if things can change.

The hope of change in relationships is wrapped up in our ability to confront, admit we're wrong, and apologize. We all need to learn how to be comfortable with all three. We're all too human to live without them.

## WHEN LIFE IS OUT OF CONTROL

I used to end my stand-up shows with a story about a time I thought I was going to get arrested. It happened one night when none of my friends were available to hang out. I was alone and bored, so I decided to go for a drive.

I was wandering down random roads when I realized I was close to a public park that someone told me about. Apparently, there's a little creek hidden away in the woods behind this soccer field. *That sounds cool,* I thought. *I should explore that.*

I parked.

Got out of my car.

Started walking toward the woods.

That's when I realized this was a terrible idea. It was eleven o'clock at night. I was alone. It was pitch black. I could hear the creek, but I couldn't see it. I thought to myself, *Man, I wish I had a light.* Right when I thought that A BRIGHT LIGHT SHONE ON MY FACE. I looked over and saw a cop car shining his spotlight on my car.

I started walking back over there so I could explain what I was doing. *I'll just tell him I came out here, to the woods, by myself, late at night, to go exploring.*

Oh no.

I suddenly realized how ridiculous that sounded. There's no way he was going to believe me.

AND HE DIDN'T!

The whole time we were talking, he was looking at me like I was the world's worst liar. He must have thought I had murdered someone and was hiding the body or that I was out there smoking crack. It was not helping my case that I was acting super nervous. I always act weird with cops, so they always think I'm guilty of something. I never am. I promise. I just don't know what a cop is legally allowed to do. One could pull me over and say, "The only way you're getting out of this ticket is if you eat this shoe," and I would immediately start chomping down.

The cop took my license back to his car, leaving me standing alone, awkwardly waiting as he decided my fate. I felt like such an idiot. *Of course this is happening to me. This is what I deserve.* I had been making all sorts of stupid and thoughtless decisions that year. Something was going to bite back. I just assumed it would be consequences from my poor financial planning, or relationships, or just my general inability to not do anything right. But no. Everything was going to come crashing down because I tried exploring a park at night. Great.

The cop came back with my I.D. He didn't look happy.

"Alright," he said. "I don't believe your story, but I guess I'll let you go." Thank God. I was free.

He went to hand me my I.D., stopped, looked at me, and said, "Is everything alright?"

And

I

Started

Crying

Hard. A lot. Extreme tears. Deep emotions pouring out of me. I was broken. This cop broke me. I could tell by the look on his face he did not expect this reaction at all. You know what? Neither did I! I heard myself saying, "I'm so depressed. I'm so unhappy." I thought, *You are? I didn't know that. Why didn't you tell me before you said something to this guy?!*

Crying and embarrassed. That was me. I did find a small silver lining. *At least it's just me and this one cop. No one else has to see this.*

Right when I thought that THREE MORE COP CARS SHOWED UP. Now I was surrounded by cops trying to calm me down, but they did not come up with a game plan ahead of time, so I was getting a lot of mixed messages.

One cop said, "Hey, man. It's ok. Everything is fine. Life's great. There's no need to cry."

A different cop said, "Dude, life sucks! I cry. I cry all the time. My kids made me cry this morning!"

Another cop looked at me and said, "Are you on any medication?"

I said, "no."

He responded, "Well, maybe, you should be."

Whenever I'd tell this in my stand-up that last line would always get a big laugh. That's how I'd end my show.

Here's the problem with this story: the first time I told anyone about what happened that night was on stage in my stand-up. I didn't want to actually process what happened. I just wanted it to get a laugh. As long as it was funny, I didn't have to deal with it. When you strip the story down to the bare parts, it's a cry for help. I was alone and depressed with emotions ready to burst out of me. He was the first person who asked if I was ok and I lost it. This was rock bottom.

I turned it into a joke so I could deflect. I got to have the relief of confessing there was a problem, but I didn't have to do it in a vulnerable way. It felt nice at the moment, but it's not like this was about to lead to any real change. It was another way of ignoring the bigger problem, sweeping it under the rug with a laugh.

Life is going to have moments where it feels like things are out of control. It could be tragedies, struggles with mental health, doubts, confusion, or any other type of suffering we face.

You make yourself vulnerable when you tell someone you feel like you're drowning.

To admit you need help.

To unload on a friend about your heartbreak.

You feel ridiculous because you've followed Christ your whole life. You know the Bible better than anyone. How is it that this diagnosis has you questioning if God is really there? But you are. That's ok. That's where you are right now.

We are not designed to walk through storms alone. Remember that the apostle Paul says we are to bear each other's burdens. You are not supposed to carry that weight on your own. Don't do what I did, and pretend like it's not really there.

It is.

God has given you the church to be there to pick it up.

You can let down your defenses.

## OUR DREAMS AND FUTURE

I saved this one for last because I thought it was a nice break from the heavier topics in this chapter. This is the only one where we're not dealing with anything negative.

It's all positive here, baby. Hooray!

Have you ever had a dream for the future that you were too embarrassed to share?

Maybe even right now you've got this itch in the back of your mind for something you want to do in life.

You want to start a nonprofit.

You feel like you should get more involved in your church.

You've been writing songs for years, and you want to release them.

You know you need to lose weight and get healthy.

You want to go back to college.

You want to adopt a child.

You want to adopt a puppy.

You want to adopt a highway.

The reason we don't say any of these dreams out loud because WHAT WILL PEOPLE THINK?! We avoid it because we have to make ourselves vulnerable to say it out loud. It's terrifying; we quit before we even try.

I had an interesting conversation with friends about my list of vulnerable moments. Several of them said they'd instead open up about any of the other ones over talking about dreams.

At first, I was so confused. I thought there was no way they really believed that. Some of those other ones are so much scarier to me. But I think I understand now. Most of the other vulnerable moments have to deal with responding to when life happens to you, things out of your control are happening. This one is the opposite. With your dreams, you're putting yourself out there. You want to make something happen. You're being proactive and saying *I think this is what my life should look like.* You can get really critical of yourself. Who are you to think you can do that? Do you even deserve it? There's no way.

Mister Rogers was right: if it's mentionable, it's manageable. If you can talk about your dreams, you can pursue them. When you say it out loud, it feels more real. And if you open up to someone you trust, their encouragement can be the motivation you need. They'll also be there to keep you accountable.

I remember when I first started telling people I was writing a book (THIS ONE!). I felt ridiculous every time I said it out loud. It's an embarrassing sentence to come out of your mouth. Who am I to write a book? But I said it. It was out there. People knew. They could check up on me. "How's the book going?" That meant I had to actually go through with it. You have no idea how big of a boost it was any time a friend said out of nowhere, "Hey man, I can't wait to read your book." It was the best feeling in the world. You would not be reading this right now if I had never admitted my dream out loud. Trustworthy people helped me make this thing a reality.

Expired dreams get moldy and turn into regrets. There is hope that things can change. The first step of vulnerability will set you on the path toward your goal.

What are you dreaming about? Where do you think God is leading you? Who can you tell?

\* \* \*

Vulnerability isn't just for rock bottom.

It's not just for someone else.

It shows up in all of our lives. We need it. It's the first step to change.

It's for you.

It's for me.

It's for today.

It's for the rest of our lives.

It leads to change!

We need to keep our eyes open for opportunities to be in the altogether in the everyday.

## REFLECTION QUESTIONS

Out of the five vulnerable moments described in the chapter (being wrong, apologizing, confrontation, when your life is out of control, and your dreams for the future) which is the scariest to you? Why?

Have you ever received an ineffective apology? What made it so bad? Have you ever given a bad apology? Did you know it was bad as you were giving it?

What is something small you're looking forward to in the next month? What is something big you're looking forward to in the next year? Five years?

# CHAPTER 5

# WHY WE HIDE

*[On Shame]*

"The lengths that we go to to put so much distance between us is staggering"

Listener, *You Were a House on Fire*

Why is it so scary to be vulnerable with someone? Why do we hide parts of ourselves? What are we risking by opening up?

Before I tell you this story, there are a few things you need to know. (1) It's a long one. Buckle up. It's worth it. (2) It's all true. I promised this really happened. (3) All names have been changed to protect identities. (4) No one got hurt.

It was the summer before my last semester of college. I was living in an apartment a few minutes down the road from campus. School was out, so all my friends were gone. My college town always turned into a ghost town during the summer. Usually, I'd be gone too, traveling with a ministry team that worked youth camps, but I stepped away my senior year. It's a good thing I did because I got to be in the right place at the right time.

I got a call from Allison, one of the leaders of the ministry team I left. Something strange was going on, and she needed my help. She gave me an address in town and asked if I could figure out who lived there. Yes. Of course. She had picked the right person for the job. I love snooping. I love secrets. I love being sneaky. I'd make an incredible private investigator. But why this address?

Allison tells me that another girl on the team, Jennifer, got the weirdest Facebook message earlier that day. A girl from her dorm reached out—totally out of nowhere— and said: "Hey, I've got those socks you needed." Jennifer had no idea what she meant.

"What are you talking about?" she responded.

"The socks you needed for that scavenger hunt. You messaged me from your ministry team's Facebook page saying you guys were doing a scavenger hunt and one of the items you needed was someone else's socks."

Jennifer was very confused. She never sent that message. There was no scavenger hunt. The team wasn't even in town. They did some snooping on their own, probably not as good as I would have done, but good enough to learn that the scavenger hunt messages actually came from a different Facebook account that was made to look identical to the ministry team's page. There was an imposter out there.

But why? WHY?! Was this some weird prank? Probably not. The imposter gave very clear instructions, including where to drop the socks off. So whoever they were they genuinely did want those socks, and they were willing to put on an elaborate scam to get them. First of all, we can assume this is a guy, right? Second, there's no wholesome reason to trick a girl into giving you their socks; he's not donating them to a shelter.

We didn't know what this guy's full plan was and frankly, we didn't want to know. All we cared about was finding out who it was and telling him to stop it.

This clearly wasn't some criminal mastermind because the dummy gave away his actual address. *We know where you live, dude!*

It turned out to be an apartment complex. I showed up under cover of night, not really sure what I was supposed to do next. *Do I need to wear a disguise? What am I trying to do here?*

I found the imposter's apartment number, and that's when I cracked this case wide open. Parked right outside was a car I recognized. The make, model, color, and unique bumper stickers all clicked in my mind. *Dexter Lemon lives here.* Of course. He's the perfect suspect. He used to be on that ministry team. And, if we're honest, and I feel like I can because I'm not using his real name, he had a history of making girls uncomfortable. I'll just say it wasn't surprising to learn that he was in the business of collecting girls' socks.

But what could we do with this information? He didn't go to our school anymore, so it's not like he could get in trouble for this. Maybe it was just a one-time thing? We intercepted the girl before he could get his hands on those socks. We thought he might give up on the whole scheme.

NOPE!

That next semester at least two more girls were contacted by the fake Facebook page. Same scheme. "We're doing a scavenger hunt, and we need your socks." We thought it was over. Everyone on the team had reported the fake page hoping Facebook would take it down. We all messaged the page saying, "Hey, stop it. We know what you're doing. You're creeping people out."

You'd think that would be enough.

The page just blocked us.

No one knew what to do. We didn't know anyone who was still in contact with Dexter or had his phone number. It felt too extreme to confront him at his apartment. It would be so easy to deny.

Luckily, things really did die down after that. A whole semester went by without any more reports of girls getting contacted. The sock scavenger hunt appeared to be over. Maybe he finally had all the socks he needed to last him a lifetime.

We were wrong. Little did we know the Sockpocalypse was coming.

One night, months later, I got on Facebook to discover a post from an old college friend. It was a long and angry rant. In the few minutes after it was posted there were already tons of comments.

The post was from a husband furious about this fake Facebook account claiming to be a traveling ministry team from his old college. He said this account messaged his wife asking for pictures of her in knee-high socks for a scavenger hunt. This husband wanted answers. He wanted consequences. He wanted to know what creep was responsible for this.

Can we just pause for a second to be in awe of the absolute boldness required to escalate this scam all the way up to *Hey, can I get pictures of you in knee-high socks? Don't worry, it's not weird, I'm doing a scavenger hunt!*

At the bottom of this husband's post were a lot of comments. I couldn't believe what I was seeing.

"I got a message like that too."

"Me too."

"Yeah. I got one of those."

"I got a message like that last month."

"They asked me for dirty socks."

And then things took a turn.

"I got the exact same message last year, but it wasn't from a fake account, it was from Dexter Lemon."

"Yeah. I got one from Dexter."

"Me too."

"Same."

It was madness. Not only was everyone calling Dexter out and sharing screenshots of his messages but they were TAG-GING HIM IN THE COMMENTS! That means he'd get notifications that people were talking about him. I can't imagine what it must have felt like for him to get online and see those comments for the first time. This secret scam you've apparently been pulling off for years is now being called out in public. You're exposed. Everyone knows this weird thing about you that you never thought would be made public. And people were not going easy on him.

Eventually Dexter tried to get involved and defend himself. It did not go well. First, he tried claiming there really was a scavenger hunt. It's all legit. He's been playing with a group of friends for a long time. How dare you not believe him!

But, like, come on. That's ridiculous. If this is real, I have so many questions.

Is this one long game you've been playing for years?

How many pairs of girls' socks do you need before you win?

What were the other items on the list?

Was it all sock related? If so, WHY?!

Who is choosing the items for this game?!

Also, I've never met anyone in my life who would be this dedicated to a scavenger hunt. Is there a prize? Is the prize that you get to keep all the socks?

Let's pretend for a second that his story was real. Why not have the other people playing with you come forward and vouch for you? His response to that was something along the lines of, "I've instructed them all not to come forward. I don't want you to treat them the same way you're treating me. I'd rather protect them!"

When that didn't work, he jumped to his second defense: "If you don't stop talking about me, I'm going to sue you," which is precisely what an innocent person would say next.

No one bought Dexter's threats. Some continued to make fun of him. Others genuinely tried to reason with him. By the end of the night, he had blocked most of us on social media. None of us ever heard from him after that night. From what I could tell he just sort of went away, never contacting anyone from our school again.

The Sockpocalypse was so strange to watch. I've been on social media for a long time. Sure, I've seen celebrities get their dirty laundry exposed and discussed online, but I've never seen it happen to someone I knew personally.

Can you imagine if that happened to you? Some weird secret gets exposed. Something private, personal, embarrassing, or inappropriate gets shared openly on the internet. It would be horrifying.

I know how evil I can be in the safety of my own head. I know the choices I've made. Some stuff I've done is plain stupid while other things in my past are pretty awful. I've worked really hard to keep the vulnerable part of my life hidden away. I'm sure you have too. Can you imagine logging on to Facebook and seeing everyone in your life openly discussing something about you that you never wanted people to know? It would be a living nightmare.

The crazy thing is that this is happening all over the internet.

Jon Ronson interviewed people who found themselves in similar situations for his book, *So You've Been Publicly Shamed*. They made an inappropriate joke online, or a scandal came out in the news. Their name became a trending topic on Twitter, and the whole internet piled on. Ronson describes telling a man at a party about some of the people he's been interviewing. Like, there was this author who was exposed for lying about sources and making up quotes in a book he published. When a journalist started digging around, asking for proof of these quotes, the author panicked and lied. He tried to cover it up, but it didn't work. The journalist reported the truth and the author's book, reputation, and entire career was ruined the moment the article was published.

Usually, when Ronson relays these stories at parties, it's with a hint of delight at how ridiculous the whole thing is.

There was something different about this story. He felt himself shuddering at the thought of the entire thing. This one was scarier.

The man Ronson spoke to knew why. Deep inside of us hides a fear—the terror of being found out.

Ronson explains:

> He meant that we all having ticking away within us something we fear will badly hurt our reputation if it got out...I think he's right. Maybe our secret is actually nothing horrendous. Maybe nobody would even consider it a big deal if it was exposed. But we can't take that risk. So we keep it buried. Maybe it's a work impropriety. Or maybe it's just a feeling that at any moment we'll blurt something out during some important meeting that'll prove to everyone that we aren't professional people or, in fact, functional human beings.[1]

Have you ever felt that terror before? That looming fear that there's something in your past, your thoughts, your struggles that, if it ever came out, would cause you to lose everything? You'd have to move far away and start your life over. Deep down, you know there's no way the people in your life would ever be able to look at you the same way again.

This is exactly how the author Brene Brown defines shame: "The fear of disconnection." It's the whisper in the back of our mind questioning, "Is there something about me that if people know it or see it, I won't be worthy of connection?"[2] This was the fear that kept me from asking for help about my taxes for so long. It stops us from apologizing, or ever admitting we're wrong. For the longest time, shame prevented me from telling anyone about my mental health struggles. I thought I couldn't talk to anyone because if I let it out my life would be over. Everyone would think I'm crazy. No one would want me around.

That's why I started this chapter with the Sockpocalypse story. It's the most extreme illustration of shame's fear coming true. There was something about Dexter that he kept hidden for so long, but when people found out it blew up. Everyone changed their minds about him. It's the worst-case scenario. It's what we fear will happen to us. Instead of opening up, we get really good at hiding. That's what shame teaches us to do. Hide.

And it's killing us.

There is a loneliness epidemic in our culture. More and more people are feeling more and more lonely. In the U.K. they've appointed a minister of loneliness whose entire role in the government is to figure out what's causing this and how to solve it. This isn't a little problem we can dismiss. Studies have found that loneliness can have the same physical effect on you as smoking 15 cigarettes a day.[3] It's affecting our hearts and our health.

Loneliness is killing us.

It's important to understand that loneliness is not the same as social isolation, which is determined by the number of people in your life. If you live on a mountain, only talk to two people all year, and your best friend is a goat then you're socially isolated (and you sound pretty cool). Loneliness, on the other hand, has nothing to do with how many people are in your life. You can be incredibly social, with thirty friends you talk to every week, heavily involved in work and church, and still feel lonely. You can be married and be lonely.

Loneliness is not about the number of people, it's about the quality of connection you have with them. Do the people in your life really know you? They might know a little, just enough to be friendly, but does anyone know you 100%?

Who knows your history?

Who knows what you've been worrying about all month?

One of the most significant contributors to our loneliness is our phones. We believe a lie about our phones and relationships that we don't believe in any other area of our life. An experience you have through a screen is not the same as having it in person. We know that's true when it comes to most things.

If you watch the Super Bowl on your phone, you do not have the same experience as the people watching it live. When you're in the stadium, it's so loud and crazy. You're surrounded by all those people. There's energy and excitement. Your heart is pounding, and people are screaming their heads off. It's not the same watching it at home. You're lying on your couch, covered in Cheeto dust. You might give out a little "woo," but that's probably just gas.

If you go to a concert, you're going to have a much better experience than all the people who stay home and end up watching the whole thing on your Instagram story. I still don't understand why people do this. Why are you posting so many videos whenever you go to a concert? Stop it.

Who is it for? The camera is shaky, the audio is terrible, and you're a million miles from the stage. Beyonce is a tiny blur. I'm not at home, jumping around and shouting, "GET IT BEYONCE! GET IT GIRL!"

An experience through a screen is not the same as having it in person. Why don't we think about that when it comes to relationships? Well, at least most of us don't. Anyone who has had family overseas in the military knows how true it is. Even though they stay connected through technology, it's not the same. You email, text, video chat whenever you can, but it's nothing like having them here in the flesh. You get to "see" them, but there's such a rush of emotion when they finally return home. You have them here, face to face, and it's so much better.

Are we relying too much on our screens for relationships?

The main criticism against social media is that no one is really sharing their real life online. People only post their highlights. Everything we share is planned, posed, and on purpose.

But shouldn't it be?

My parents still have photo albums under the coffee table in their living room. You know what it's full of? Highlights! Posed pictures! They kept the best shots from weddings, birthdays, and vacations. That's what photo albums were made for. No one flips through one and says, *Why aren't there any pictures where you look sad and ugly?* Social media is the new photo album.

You'd also never see someone hand you a photo album and say, *This is everything you need to know about me.* No one would believe that. There's so much more than highlights. The problem isn't how we're using it but how much we're using it. We're trying to crawl inside a photo album and pretend we can live in it. We're not meant to live our whole lives on the internet. The reason we're upset at social media for not being more raw and honest is that we're not getting that anywhere else in life. It's like going to Olive Garden and complaining that there aren't any showers. That's not what this place is for. You're supposed to be getting that somewhere else.

Social media wasn't built to handle vulnerability. Have you ever seen a friend post something really personal online? It doesn't feel right. We immediately question their motives. *It looks like they're just trying to get attention.*

Maybe that's part of the reason we like to have all of our relationships through a screen. It's easier. We're able to keep relationships shallow. We can lurk in group messages, follow friends from a distance, and no one has to really know us. The internet is the perfect place to hide.

It's risky to open up!

You don't know how people are going to respond. There's a chance the next thing you reveal about yourself is what makes people change their minds about you. Why risk it? Just keep people away, and you'll never get hurt. But that's shame talking. Shame is wrapped up in our loneliness issue, it's what keeps us from vulnerability, and it limits our relationship with God.

Sin separates us from God; shame traps us in hiding. We see this in the Bible all the way back in Genesis 3. After Adam and Eve eat the fruit, they realize the huge mistake they've made and feel like they need to hide. They hide from each other by covering up with makeshift clothes. Then, when they hear God approaching, they try to hide from Him too. Which, if we're honest, is a pretty dumb plan. First of all, He's going to find you. Obviously. It's the worst game of hide and seek. He knows where you are. Secondly, what's the end goal? It's a short term solution. Do they really think they can hide forever? That's not much of a life.

They hide for the same reason any of us hide: they're afraid of how God will react.

Shame kicks in, making them think they have to protect themselves. It's too dangerous to be in the altogether. Why risk being exposed? If your walls are down if you're out in the open, there's a chance there's something about you that will make people change their minds about you.

Eventually, Adam and Eve come out of hiding and stand before God. They explain everything and wait for God's response. This is the moment they feared.

What will God do?

He could turn his back on them. Reject them. Destroy them. This could be the last time He ever speaks to them.

No.

His first words are love. The first message he has for Adam and Eve is I'm going to fix this. He speaks to the serpent who deceived and tempted Eve:

> The Lord God said to the serpent,
> "Because you have done this,
> cursed are you above all livestock
> and above all beasts of the field;
> on your belly you shall go,
> and dust you shall eat
> all the days of your life.
> I will put enmity between you and the woman,
> and between your offspring and her offspring;
> he shall bruise your head,
> and you shall bruise his heel. (Genesis 3:14-15)"

God is saying, *Sin has separated man from me, but through a descendant of Eve, I will bring reconciliation.* Do you know who that is? Do you know who God is promising? It's Jesus. Genesis 3:15 is known as the protoevangelium, the first gospel. It's the first time Jesus is mentioned in the Bible. That's how God responds. He doesn't turn his back. He offers hope.

He says, *I see you. Things might be bad, but something good is coming. I'm not giving up. I'm not going away.*

We don't have to hide from God. We don't have to be afraid of his response. It's Jesus. It's love. And the great thing about God is that He doesn't change. You can't surprise Him with something you're hiding. There is nothing in your life that would make Him change His mind about you. If His answer was Jesus once, it always is. Every time. The hundredth time. The thousandth time. Even with that (whatever that is for you). Even when you've been following Christ your whole life, and you should "know better." His answer is Jesus five seconds after you fall, and it's still Jesus five years after.

Obviously, this isn't how everyone responds to our vulnerability. You see that in the Sockpocolypse story. I know I've had times I've tried to open up to a friend and they responded with the dumbest and most insensitive comments. It hurt. I hated it. That's why at the end of that Mister Rogers' quote ("if it's mentionable it can be more manageable") he says, "The people we trust with that important talk can help us know that we are not alone." With a lot of vulnerable conversations, we can choose who we open up to, so we should find the people we can trust.

Shame tells us that no one is safe. Shame is also a liar who is more concerned with you, presenting yourself as likable, spotless, and perfect. Shame wants you to hide behind the photo album you're living in online, pretending to already be the ideal version of who you want to be. But that's a miserable way to live, leaving you lonely, not really connecting with the people in your life.

In a commencement speech from 2011, author Jonathan Franzen spoke to the graduating class of Kenyon College about the problem of wanting to be likable. He said that when that becomes your ultimate goal in life, "you've despaired of being loved for who you really are."[4] You put out this filtered, curated, likable version of yourself other people can only access through a screen, and it might work really well. You might trick a lot of people to love that version of yourself, but it will never really satisfy you. Compliments become meaningless. They say you're such a kind person and all you can think is *yeah, that's because you don't actually know me.*

You want to know what vulnerability feels like? Unlock your phone and hand it to someone. Give them full access. Sit back and watch them go through everything. For most people, that would be an absolute nightmare. You don't even have to have anything inappropriate or some big terrible secret for it to feel risky. They could see the embarrassing search history from the last time you were sick. They might find the hundred ugly selfies you took before you found the perfect one you posted. They could read the immature, passive-aggressive text fight you got into last week. They could see the playlist of old love songs you made for the first date you went on three years ago with the girl who eventually rejected you. *Why do you still have that, Taylor?*

The fear is that there is something worth hiding.

So we hide. We put on a show, and we hate it when people are fooled.

The only relationships that will truly defeat our culture's loneliness epidemic are ones where can be fully known AND fully loved.

Pastor Tim Keller speaks about this kind of love:

> To be loved but not known is comforting but superficial. To be known and not loved is our greatest fear.

> But to be fully known and truly loved is, well, a lot like being loved by God. It is what we need more than anything. It liberates us from pretense, humbles us out of our self-righteousness, and fortifies us for any difficulty life can throw at us.[5]

We don't have to fear what God will say when we step into the light. His first response will always be Jesus, the source of all our hope. He knows us fully and loves us fully. That's the kind of love that frees us to fight back against our shame.

We think we need to put up walls to protect ourselves. We get so caught up on what the walls will keep from getting out — our secrets and our shame— that we never notice all the things it stops from getting in— real love, deep relationships, and the hope for change.

The best way to defeat shame is to share it. Brene Brown says, "Shame hates it when we reach out and tell our story. It hates having words wrapped around it—it can't survive being shared. Shame loves secrecy."[6] It might feel risky to take that first step out of hiding, but it gets easier. Shame keeps us from being vulnerable, but vulnerability keeps us from dwelling in our shame.

In the story of Adam and Eve, we don't get a sense of how long they hid from God before they got to hear the promise of Jesus. No matter how short or long it was, you just know it was not a fulfilling way to live.

How could you possibly focus on anything except keeping a good hiding place?

If it were me, I wouldn't have been able to stop picturing how angry God would be if He ever found me. That would only serve to fuel the panic and make me want to hide even more. Then He'd eventually find me, fully see me, and still fully love me. Instead of words of hate, He'd tell me about Jesus. There'd be a great sense of relief from that, but I'm sure I'd also be frustrated with how long I spent in hiding. I put my life and my relationship with God on pause for that entire time. I could have spent it with Him, getting closer. I didn't have to hide. He was always going to tell me about Jesus.

We must recognize that this is what we are prone to do. The fear of shame drags us into hiding. When we understand that it's easier to notice it when it's happening. We can stop ourselves and say *Wait a second. What am I doing? This isn't me making this decision. This is my shame, talking.* Then we can fight back.

## REFLECTION QUESTIONS

How has social media affected your relationships?

How does shame stop us from growing in our relationship with Christ?

What are topics we keep hidden in the church because we're afraid they're shameful? What are some ways we could talk about, bring to light, or deal with those topics?

# CHAPTER 6

# AND YET

*[On Grace]*

"Take heart, my son; your sins are forgiven."

Jesus, *Matthew 9:2*

So far, we've talked about why vulnerability is essential in the life of a Christian, why it can be scary, and we uncovered the true identity of the anti-Christ (just kidding). Now we'll spend the next two chapters looking at why we don't have to be afraid to open up to God and His church.

In the Gospel of John, we read the story of a woman who shows up to her town's well at noon. To us, that might not sound weird, but in the culture of that time, no one went for water at noon. You'd go early in the morning or later in the day. Noon was the hottest time of day. It was too miserable to go then. When we read about this woman showing up when no one else would be there, we can assume she's probably trying to avoid people.

Her plan doesn't work, though, because Jesus is already hanging out at the well. He's been on a ministry trip with his disciples and they decided to take a pit stop in this Samaritan town. Everyone else went off to get lunch, but Jesus hung back, alone at the well.

Jesus strikes up a conversation with the woman, which really freaks her out. Why would he talk to her? He should consider her an outcast in every sense of the word. First off, she's a Samaritan. Jesus is Jewish. Jews despised Samaritans, often going to great lengths to avoid them. Second, she's a woman, and in that society that made her a second class citizen, less than a man. She could assume this Jewish man would consider her beneath Him. Then there's whatever drama is going on that makes her want to avoid the crowds. You know how small towns are. Everyone knows everyone's business.

None of that mattered to Jesus.

She doesn't know what to say when Jesus asks her for a drink of water. He continues, "If you knew the gift of God and who it is saying to you, 'give me a drink,' you would have asked him, and he would have given you living water."

Jesus goes on to explain how this living water is unique.

Everyone who drinks of this water will be thirsty again, but whoever drinks of the water I will give him will never be thirsty again. The water that I will give him will become in him a spring of water welling up for eternal life.

He says drinking from any other well won't be able to fully satisfy. You'll always need to go back for another drink, but the water He's offering is different. You'll never need to look for another drink again.

When the woman asks for this water, Jesus says, "Go and get your husband." She says she doesn't have one, and Jesus tells her He already knew that. Jesus reveals that she's actually had five husbands and now she's living with a man she isn't married to. Sounds pretty scandalous, doesn't it? If you had someone in your small town who kept getting married over and over, word would probably spread. She might feel uncomfortable in public and try to hide. The shame could be too much, pressing down from the community judging her. She doesn't get any of that from Jesus, only the offer of living water.

Why did Jesus even bring up her husband in the first place if He knows she doesn't have one? It sounds so random. Is Jesus saying she's not allowed to have a drink unless she gets permission from the man in her life? No!

If we break down what "living water" means in the simplest terms, Jesus is offering a relationship with Him. He's inviting her into the kingdom of Heaven, the family of God. Jesus says that relationship will satisfy like no other can. She says she wants in, so He points out the thing in her life where she was searching for satisfaction: marriage.

Finding a husband was her source of hope. She thought *something good is coming if I just get married.* But it doesn't work. It doesn't satisfy so she goes back to the well. *OK. Nothing is changing, so it must not be this marriage.* She finds a new husband. *This will change everything.* It doesn't. A third marriage. A fourth. A fifth. She has to keep going back to the well. Finally, she decides to skip the wedding and just move in with a guy.

Jesus wants to show her that He is the true source of hope. If she wants everything to change, it's only through Him. He offers her this living water.

The woman is amazed by how Jesus is speaking. She's heard all of the prophecies of the coming savior. The way Jesus is talking about Himself makes her think this might really be Him.

"I who speak to you am He," Jesus says.

He's here.

This conversation really blows her away. As the disciples are coming back from lunch, she runs off into town to tell everyone about Jesus. Moments ago, this woman was doing whatever it took to avoid the people in her town, but now something in her has changed.

The way John writes it, the main thing the woman tells the town about Jesus is, "He told me all I ever did."[1] On the surface, it sounds like she's in awe of his miraculous knowledge but isn't it more than that? This small town is probably full of people who could tell her everything she ever did. But Jesus knew her life, **AND YET** He still spoke to her. Jesus knew her past. He knew her mistakes. He saw her brokenness, **AND YET** He still offered her love and living water. This man is the much-anticipated hope sent by God, and she was a nobody samaritan, **AND YET**. She was an outcast, she had five failed marriages, she was a screw-up, **AND YET**. That's the part that shocked her.

"**AND YET**" is the whole story of the gospel.

"**AND YET**" is grace.

We have to be careful about how we deal with our shame. It can get messy because there's truth tangled up in the lies our shame tells us. It's true that when we are the lord of our own life, we hurt ourselves and others, disrupting the great big beautiful picture God is orchestrating in the world. It's true that we are sinful and, left to our own devices, capable of evil. The reward for a life apart from God is indeed death. A Christian's shame is not defeated by downplaying the severity of our sin. It's not a message of *it's OK to come out of hiding because you're not really a bad person.*

Shame dies with the message of **AND YET**. Sometimes the problem of shame is not that we're overestimating how broken we are, but we're underestimating how powerful God's grace is. The protoevangelium is the first "**AND YET**" of scripture. Despite everything we have done to try to prove how unlovable we are, God will not let go.

The grace of God means we do not get what we deserve. That's a message I was able to celebrate recently in an unexpected place.

I found out I was preaching my grandpa's funeral an hour before it started. A snowstorm hit the night before, and when we woke up in the morning, there were about nine inches of snow on the ground. An hour before the service was set to start the minister called my mom to say his car was trapped in his driveway, and he had no way of getting out. My mom pulled me aside to tell me the news.

"If he can't make it who is going to speak?" I asked.

"You are."

I don't know if I'm a good enough writer to convey just how casually she said this. Like this was always the plan. It wasn't. This was the first I heard anything about it. I was in shock. This was my own nightmare Diet Coke commercial, and my mom was saying, "Look, here's the thing about you speaking at your grandpa's funeral."

I spent that hour in the back of the funeral home frantically writing. I had never preached a funeral before.

What are the rules?

What am I allowed to say?

I freaked out for a few minutes, but when I finally calmed down, I realized this might be the easiest funeral to preach. My grandpa's life is the perfect story of grace.

My grandpa, Morton Galoskowsky (I promise that's his real name and not the result of a cat walking across my keyboard), passed away at the age of ninety. For the majority of his life, he did not follow Christ. He'd go to church with my grandma every week, but he never believed. For as long as I can remember, my family was trying to convince my grandpa to follow Christ. We'd always pray and talk to him about it whenever we got the chance. In the fourth grade, I sent him a book that explained salvation with a note that said, "Please give all of this some thought."

He was never open to any of it until he was eighty years old. That was the year he gave his life to Jesus and was baptized.

At his funeral, I preached Matthew 2:1-16, the parable of the laborers in the vineyard. Jesus says the kingdom of Heaven is like a landowner who needs some work done in his fields. He goes out early in the morning, finds workers, and says he'll pay them each one denarius for a day's work. Later in the day, the landowner goes out for more workers. Even later, he finds some more. Close to the end of the day, he sees a few more who can work. When the day is over, he pays each the same wage. Even those who didn't start working until there were only a few hours left received the same reward as those who worked since dawn. This angers the workers who were hired first. The landowner responds, "Friend, I am doing you no wrong; did you not agree with me for a denarius? Take what is yours and go, but I wish to give to this last man the same as you. Is it not lawful for me to do what I wish with what is my own? Or is your eye envious because I am generous?"

Jesus is aiming this parable at the religious leaders of His time who looked on in frustration as Jesus taught that the kingdom of Heaven was for everyone. Gentiles, sinners, and all those far from God were welcomed to have a seat at the table. Those religious leaders believe their ability to hold to their own rules meant they deserved a greater reward than the rest.

If those religious leaders had it their way, my grandpa wouldn't have gotten a very warm welcome into Heaven. His reward would have been small and unimpressive. After all, he only followed Christ for the last ten years of his life, and it's not like he did any big important ministry in that time. He spent most of those years dealing with memory loss. Both his mind and body were getting weaker, so he didn't feel comfortable leaving the house much. Sometimes it was a miracle he made it in time for church on Sunday morning.

AND YET...

According to this parable, my grandfather walked into Heaven to the same reception and celebration as the apostle Paul, Zacchaeus, and the Samaritan woman at the well. My grandpa did not get what he deserved. He was given a gift of love by our Father. He didn't earn it. He didn't prove himself worthy of the reward. The religious leaders would say, *That's not fair!* and God would reply, *You're right, but that's grace.*

The good news of the gospel is that, on the cross, Jesus took on everything that you deserve. Shame tells you to stay hidden, put on a costume, never breaking character. Shame will say you've messed up too many times and you don't deserve to go to God for help. Remember that what you deserve was taken care of on the cross.

When shame says, *You need to work to prove yourself worthy before coming to God*, remember: all of the work was done on the cross.

We don't have to fear being vulnerable with God. When we open up to Him, His response will always be love. No matter how bad things get, there's always an **AND YET** waiting for you in our Father's arms.

We must open up to God, but if that's all we have, we can still find ourselves frustrated when we feel lost. With God, we don't have a face to look at while we're crying out. We can end up second-guessing how He feels about our situation because He's not standing right in front of us.

I know He loves me. I know His grace can cover everything, but when things are falling apart, I can start to doubt it all. What is He thinking up there?

In the Old Testament story of Job, we see a man who suffered the same confusion when everything good in his life was taken from him. His wealth, family, and health are all ripped away, and he's left with nothing but ashes. Job has been faithful through it all. He is desperate to know why this is all happening. Has God stopped caring about him? I'm sure this was a common struggle for anyone following God during the times of the Old Testament.

For so long God felt so far away. Until one day He came down and lived among us.

Jesus comes to Earth and not only does He fulfill His purpose as the sacrifice we need, He also comes to be the face of God. Finally, people get to see tangible reactions from God.

The people of Israel no longer had to doubt if God cared when they suffered. They saw Jesus at the tomb of Lazarus weeping with the family. Jesus had already said He going to raise Lazarus from the dead, so there was no reason to cry, but He was still brought to tears when He saw how much the people were hurting. He joined them in their suffering. We get to see that God cares.

The outcasts no longer had to question if God even knew who they were because they saw Jesus surround Himself with the poor, lowly, and ignored. There's a special place of honor in His company for them. If it's true for Jesus, it's true for the Father.

But here's the problem: at the end of his ministry on Earth Jesus leaves, returning to Heaven. What are we supposed to do now that we don't have Him walking among us anymore? We can always go back to the gospels and remind ourselves of what Jesus did, but I know in my life, I can still run into doubts. If I'm not careful, my shame can overwhelm me, and I can talk myself out of believing the same Jesus of the Bible is on the other end of my prayers.

I know Jesus forgives sins. I know even Peter, the disciple who was constantly screwing up, is loved and never abandoned, but what if that doesn't apply to me? What if I've wasted so much of God's time that He's ready to give up on me? I've given the same speech about how *this time is going to be different!* I just picture God rolling his eyes. He really doesn't believe me, and neither do I. I feel so stupid. I should give up. I shouldn't even bother God with this.

The good news is that Jesus didn't leave us here on our own. The Holy Spirit came to live in Jesus' followers, doing the work of making them more like Him. Christians are to live as Christ's ambassadors (2 Cor. 5:20), representing who Jesus is for the world. They are called to bear Christ's image, acting as a mirror to reflect Jesus' character.

Here's how it's supposed to be: the way a Christian looks at you is the way Jesus looks at you. The way a Christian forgives, loves, and cares for you is showing off the way Jesus does as well. Whenever you feel yourself doubting God in your vulnerable moments, you can always turn to the church for the reassurance that Jesus has not given up on you.

It feels weird to write that because I'm a Christian and I know I'm not always doing a good job representing Jesus. I have a lot of bad days where if a stranger had to describe who Jesus is based on their interactions with me, I'd be humiliated. They'd think Jesus must be a jerk. But He's not! That's why apologies are such a critical part of our lives as Christians. We're not always going to do a good job living like Jesus. We'll fall short. We're going to be impatient or do something we shouldn't. We need to be willing to then say, "I'm sorry for what I did. That does not represent who Jesus is, and that's not how I want to act. Please forgive me. I want to do better." Can you imagine if your church had the kind of culture where that was a regular practice? It would be incredible. Everyone would be so open and honest and working to show off Jesus to each other. We need that.

It's always been difficult for Christians to show each other the grace Jesus has for them. In the New Testament, we can read a letter the apostle Paul wrote for the Galatian church to address leaders who were adding on more requirements for people who wanted to join the church. These leaders wanted to make others prove themselves. There was more work to be done to earn a spot in the body of Christ. Paul writes to remind the church that all of the work needed for salvation is complete. Jesus already did it.

Grace is incredibly tough for us to comprehend. We can't wrap our minds around it. For me, that actually strengthens my belief in the gospel. How could this be a man-made religion? Grace is so foreign to us. Other religions will either get rid of any need for it by teaching that things aren't really that bad, or they replace grace with works. Earn it. Work for the reward. Get what you deserve. The grace of Christ sounds ridiculous to us. It makes no sense. Why would the creator of the universe offer this gift? Our flesh can't handle that message. It sounds too good to be true, so we feel like we can't trust it. We add to the gospel, changing it, to better fit what we think we actually deserve.

Imagine you've just bought a house. It's a fixer-upper. You've never really done any home improvement before, but you're sure you can figure it out. After a month of working, you realize you've made a colossal mistake. The place is a disaster. You tried to install new pipes, but they burst when you turned the water on, now the downstairs is flooded. You thought it would be nice to knock down a wall to make the master bedroom a little bigger, but it turns out that was a load-bearing wall, and now part of the roof is caving in. You rewired the light switches and started an electrical fire that blew off your eyebrows and almost burned down the whole kitchen.

You have no idea what you're going to do now. The house is barely standing. It's not safe to sleep there. It's hardly safe to look at. You have nowhere to live. All of your money went into this project. You're broke. You can't afford to fix this.

One day at church you're talking about it with a group of friends. You're choking back tears because the whole situation is overwhelming. You can't sleep or eat. It's all you can think about.

"I can help." You didn't even notice that this man was listening to your story. He explains that he's new to the church and he owns a construction company. He offers to send a team to work on your house. You decline the offer and tell him you would have no way to pay for it.

"We'll figure something out."

You don't know what that means but you're too embarrassed to ask. There's also a part of you that doesn't think this guy is actually serious about helping. It's just a nice thing to say. There's no way he'll actually follow through.

The next day you drive by your disaster house on your way to work. You've been staying in a hotel as you figure out what to do next, but you've been visiting it every morning just to guarantee you're as stressed as you can be all day.

To your surprise, when you pull up to the house, you see dozens of construction workers already hard at work. For the next several days you see progress you didn't even think was possible. By the end of the week, it's a totally different house. They must have been working all through the night.

When the owner of the company gives you a tour of the finished product, you feel like you're going to pass out. It's beautiful, even greater than what you were hoping. A celebrity could live here. You recognize how expensive different elements of the house are. You remember seeing those light fixtures when you were shopping around. You know how much those doors would have cost. Everything is way out of your price range.

By the end of the tour, you're no longer able to appreciate what they've done, you're too distracted adding up how much all of this is going to cost. You don't have this kind of money. You don't have any kind of money.

As the owner of the company leads you to the front door, one of his employees approaches you with the bill. Your heart stops beating. It's more than you'll make in ten years. It's probably more than you'll ever make in your entire life. You don't know what to do. The owner of the company takes the bill away from you and says he's going to pay for it.

Your heart stops again. You've never had a heart attack before, but maybe this is what it feels like.

Why would he pay for all of this? You got yourself into this mess, you wrecked the house. It's your fault. You should be the one to fix it. Plus, this guy barely knows you.

Why would he give you this?

A few nights later, you're staying in your brand new home. You keep playing that moment over and over in your head. Maybe you misread it? Maybe this is just a loan? That would make more sense. He knew you couldn't pay it all off at once so he took care of it and he's expecting you to make payments over the next few years. That must be it, right? That's got to be what's happening.

That next Sunday before church, you approach him with a check. "Here's my first payment. It's not much, but it's what I have."

He doesn't take it. He just smiles at you. "You'll never be able to pay it back, and I don't want you to try. It's a gift."

You do this every Sunday for the next few weeks. You offer the check, and he turns it down every time. He tells you to stop trying to pay it back. He says it's a gift.

The question is, will you ever believe Him? Will you finally accept the gift and stop treating it like it's merely a loan?

You don't have to hide from him or avoid him until you have the money to pay him back. You don't have to pretend like you really do have the money, even though you never will.

You didn't deserve it, and yet He paid to make it new.

When our shame tells us to hide, and our God feels far away, we can look to the church to represent Jesus.

When you're overwhelmed with what you deserve, they can look at you with the eyes of Christ and remind your debt is paid off. You owe nothing.

I remember one time I opened up to a pastor about what was going on in my life, fully expecting him to yell at me all the things I had been yelling at myself. *You shouldn't be struggling like this! You went to Bible college. You should know better. YOU SHOULD KNOW BETTER.* The pause after I finished my story was one of the most tense silences of my life. My words hung in the air as I waited for how he'd respond. I braced myself for impact, but I knew it was still going to hurt.

He'd tell me how disappointed he was, that I was being stupid. At least we'd end up with a clear plan for what I needed to do next to make things right, to pay back my loan.

Then he spoke.

"Have you prayed for forgiveness?"

"Yes."

He looked me in the eye and said,

"Then, your sins are forgiven."

That was it. That was the end. It hit me like a punch in the gut. This is what grace feels like? This feels impossible. It makes no sense. How is it that easy? Why don't I have to work for this?

A weight fell off my shoulders, one that I had been trying to work off on my own, but only the cross was strong enough to free me.

Jesus did the work so I could get what I don't deserve.

When we are in Christ, there's no reason to hide. We are free. We do not have to fear moments of being in the altogether. With whatever you're afraid of sharing there's an **AND YET** waiting for you.

## REFLECTION QUESTIONS

Who in your life has represented Christ well and shown you the grace of Jesus?

Why is it so difficult for Christians to understand grace?

Why do you think grace would make us more comfortable being vulnerable?

# CHAPTER 7

# YOU'RE NOT ALONE

*[The Hope We Find in Community]*

"Friendship is born at the moment when one man says to another What! You too? I thought no one but myself..."

-C.S. Lewis, *The Four Loves*

I never complain about wifi to my grandma (nor do I complain about my grandma to my wifi). She has no idea what that is. It feels wrong to take your problems to someone who won't understand. What good will it do? All she can offer is a confused look and a lot of questions. I should save it for someone who actually uses the internet and spare my grandma from having to listen to me.

Top 3 Things I've Never Complained to my Grandma About:
1. Technology
2. How dairy gives me gas
3. Depression

Actually, for the longest time depression was on the list of things I'd never complain about to anyone. I thought I was the only one in my little world struggling with it, so I thought no one would understand. I was alone. The fear I had welling up inside of me was that if I let this out no one would know how to handle it. There was something wrong with me, and I didn't have a single person in my life who could help fix it. I was

Humpty Dumpty, and if I let myself come crashing down, all the king's horses and all the king's men would try to put me back together again, and they'd fail miserably. Even worse, maybe I didn't have any king's men at all, only horses. How are they going to put me back together? They're horses!

I thought my life was going to be stuck that way forever. Nothing would ever change. I'd carry this secret around, suffering in silence for the rest of my life. Nothing good was coming, only more of the same. But then I found out I wasn't alone.

On a summer road trip, a friend and I had to share a hotel room. While we were unpacking, he said, "I should probably just tell you this now. I take medication for depression. I just realized you're going to see it on the counter in the bathroom and I didn't want it to surprise you. So there's that."

I was shocked. My brain could not comprehend this. It was like my friend had just said, *Oh, by the way, I'm from another planet and aliens are real, and we've been watching you.* There was no sign, no warning that this could be possible. My whole understanding of the world was rocked. Someone this close to me had experienced what I was feeling? I wouldn't have guessed it was him of all people. He always seemed so...normal? Put together?

And the way he even talked about the medication threw me off. He said it so casually. Like it was no big deal. This whole time I was keeping my struggle a secret because I thought it was a VERY big deal. Too big to admit. Why wasn't he as scared as I was?

It was my first time witnessing someone live out that Mister Rogers' quote. For him, depression was mentionable, that made it more manageable.

The rest of the trip, I asked questions about his journey with mental health. It was so crazy to hear him describe what he went through because it was just like what I was currently feeling.

I wasn't alone. Not only had someone else been where I am now, but he clearly wasn't there anymore. There was hope for change in my life! It didn't always have to be like this.

After the trip, I had the courage to tell my parents about my mental health struggle for the first time. I was still nervous about being vulnerable with them, but at least I knew other people had been here before.

I remember calling my mom and saying, "I think I want to go to a doctor and see if I'd be diagnosed with depression." My mom asked why I felt that way, and I told her about a lot of my struggles over the last few years.

"Oh, I've had that," she said.

WHAT?!

"Oh yeah. I used to take medication for anxiety."

I was blown away again. There were people all around me who had been in my shoes before.

This is one of the most important things we get out of being a part of the body of Christ: stories. We get to hear the stories of people who have gone before us to let us know we're not alone.

The apostle Paul writes to Timothy about his own story:

> The saying is trustworthy and deserving of full acceptance, that Christ Jesus came into the world to save sinners, of whom I am the foremost. But I received mercy for this reason, that in me, as the foremost, Jesus Christ might display his perfect patience as an example to those who were to believe in him for eternal life. (1 Timothy 1:15-16)

All throughout his writing, Paul is so honest about his past as a sinner, far from Christ. This passage shows us why. He knows that one of the reasons God saved him was so his life could be an example for others. This is a gift to all those who have not yet come to Christ. Paul wants them to know they're not alone. He was once where they are now. It's easier to open up when you know others have been where you are.

The church should be filled with people like Paul, holding their lives up as an example for others. Often, however, shame can keep us in hiding, afraid to speak on issues the Lord has already forgiven.

Christians are often terrible at talking about porn. We won't even say its name. In the Harry Potter books, wizards are so scared of the villain, Voldermort, that they never say his name out loud. They just call him "You-Know-Who." Porn is the Voldermort of sins. We call it "stuff on the Internet." Come on. What other stuff is there on the Internet? It's PORN!

Think of what we're teaching our church if we're not willing to say the word porn. If this sin is so bad they're not willing to say it on stage, why would anyone feel comfortable opening up about their own struggle with it?

The way I hear most sermons address porn is in such a quick little comment. Usually, the pastor is talking about those who are far away from God. *Some of you are doing things you know you shouldn't. You're looking at stuff on the Internet.* That's it. Moving on. It's a vague *you're doing this, it's terrible, now stop it!* Where's the hope that things can change in Christ? Where's the empathy? Where's the hope that this person can call on God and the church to be there for them? The only message they're hearing is *you're disgusting and you need to take care of this on your own and I better not hear about it.*

We don't just have this problem with porn. There are other issues we need to learn how to talk about in church. Any controversial topic can end up being handled with little empathy if we're not careful. Have you ever heard a sermon where it sounded like the speaker was more concerned with proving they believe all the right things about an issue rather than ministering to those struggling with it? For me, the two most significant examples are abortion and sexual identity (LGBTQ+ issues).

No matter what you believe, can we all agree that there are people in every church personally connected to these issues? In the average church, there's a good chance at least one woman in your church has had an abortion. She might not be a long-standing member but any given Sunday you might have a guest who has. There's also a good chance there are people in your church struggling to figure out their sexual identity. Are we speaking to them? Do they know they are loved? Do they know that they are not alone? Do they know they can talk to someone about it? A lot of times it just feels like a pastor is preaching to the choir. They stand up and proudly proclaim, *This is where we stand on this issue.* Everyone applauds. Nothing is said to those dealing with that issue. They might feel so alone, thinking, *They must be comfortable doing this because they don't think anyone here is dealing with that. I must be the only one.*

They're not.

We need to act like it.

Shame says there's something about you that you need to hide because if people find out, they'll reject you completely. This is why it's so beautiful that the church can offer stories of other people who came out of hiding, were met with grace and love, and found hope for change in Christ. The church gets to say, *Look at these lives! They wrapped words around their issues, and it didn't destroy them. It actually made things so much better.*

When people know they're not alone, they feel more comfortable opening up. Porn is the perfect example of this. Every time the topic comes up with a group of Christian guys (I can only speak to my experience as a guy, but I don't want to pretend that men are the only ones dealing with this) it usually follows the same pattern. At first, everyone gets extremely uncomfortable. Maybe one or two say something vague about having a problem in their past, but that's about it. If someone is brave enough to take a step in and say, "I still sometimes struggle with it," then everyone else lets out a sigh of relief because they can admit that too. Then if someone goes all in

135

and says they're still dealing with it now, all the walls come down and every guy feels safe enough to join in with their own vulnerable stories. You would have never guessed it by the way the conversation started that it was an issue for so many in the group. Everyone always starts out holding their cards close to the chest. They've all been practicing their poker faces for years, fearing they were the only one with a porn problem.

We also see the power of finding out you're not alone with the #MeToo movement. Some of the men and women who shared their stories of the harassment they experienced in Hollywood waited decades to finally open up. It was when they knew others had been through something similar that they felt comfortable talking. Even the name of the movement speaks to this. What a relief to hear someone say, "Me too."

It's a powerful message, but if we're not careful we can let it lead us down two different, unhealthy paths.

The first is that there is a danger of overcorrecting. We could get so focused on the relief that comes from knowing we're not alone that we forget about the hope for change. This is how authenticity turns into a problem. Everyone comes out of hiding, proudly announcing who they really are and what they're dealing with, and we think that is comforting enough. We stop at the message that everyone is equally messed up. But there is hope. Change is possible.

God does not want to leave you where you are. Jesus came and died so you didn't have to stay where you are. The Holy Spirit lives within you so you don't have to stay where you are. He is shaping you into a witness for Christ.

Let's be clear about what the apostle Paul is saying to Timothy in the passage we looked earlier. He doesn't mean that his life is an example of just how messed up a Christian's past can be. He says his life is an example of "God's perfect patience." He's willing to hold his life up so others can see how much the gospel has changed it. It's as if he's saying, *Look at who I was and who I am now. If God can change me, of course, he can change you. If he can love me, forgive me, and transform my identity, he can do the same for you.* I wouldn't have been compelled to do something about my depression if my friend was still in the same situation as me. It would have been nice, but what's the point of trying if this guy has been dealing with it longer than me and nothing has changed for him yet?

We get examples, but they're examples of transformation.

Look at what God can do.

In *The Power of Habit*, Charles Duhigg writes about how one of the most essential ingredients needed for us to succeed in changing something about our lives is belief. We have to believe that things really can change. One of the greatest places to grow that belief is in community.

Lee Ann Kaskutas is a senior scientist at the Alcohol Research Group. She sees how Alcoholics Anonymous taps into this.

> At some point, people in AA look around the room and think if it worked for that guy I guess it can work for me. There's something really powerful about groups and shared experiences. People might be

> skeptical about their ability to change if they're by themselves, but a group will convince them to suspend disbelief. A community creates belief.[1]

There's this old story: A man is walking down the street when he falls into a hole. The walls of the hole are so high he can't climb out on his own.

A doctor walks by, and the man yells out, "Doc, I'm stuck down here. Can you help?" The doctor writes a prescription and throws it down in the hole.

Then a priest walks by. Again the man shouts, "Father, can you get me out of here?" The priest writes a prayer and tosses it in the hole.

Then a friend walks by. The man shouts, "Joe! Please. I can't get out. Can you help?" The friend jumps down in the hole with the man.

"What are you doing? Now we're both trapped in here!"

The friend replies, "Yeah, but I've been down here before— I know the way out."

I know it's scary, but if we allow ourselves to get close enough to the people in our church, we'll start to recognize similar scars and wounds to the ones we have.

You're not alone. There are people who know the way out.

There is another danger to this message: If we're not careful, we can hear, *There are people in the church who have been where you are*, and think the only way you'll find them is to look for people just like you. When you do that you rob yourself of the beautiful diversity present in the kingdom of God.

A retired married couple can look an eighteen year old in the eye and say, *You're not alone. We've been down here before, and we know the way out.* That might actually be more powerful. The teenager could assume everyone her age struggles with doubt but to hear an elder in the church hold their life up as an example could be really amazing. The CEO of a giant corporation could be in a Bible study with a poor college student and find encouragement in a testimony of God's provision in the student's life. People don't have to look exactly like you to have been where you've been.

In the church world, the longer you're single, the more people start to worry about you. As all your friends get married, you can begin to feel like a leper, forced out of the camp until you're cured. Once you find a spouse, you can come back and join the community. Until then you're pushed off to the side with all the other single people. It's so discouraging. You can end up having a lot of conversations with married friends where they keep making it perfectly clear that you have no idea how difficult it is to be married. I know it's true, but when you make that the only thing we talk about, it starts to feel like we have nothing in common. I understand there is a need to have people in your community who are in a similar stage of life. New parents need friends who are also new parents to talk about baby stuff. Empty nesters need other empty nesters. But we can't be so rooted in people just like us that we miss an opportunity to hear stories of hope from someone we wouldn't expect.

We don't have to narrow this down to just the intense vulnerable moments. We need examples of Christians who have had to apologize. We need examples of Christians who have followed God's calling. We need examples of all shapes and sizes.

Here's the coolest part: if you're going through something right now, one day you're going to be the example for someone else. You're going to be on the other side of this, talking to someone going through a dark time, and you'll get to say, *If He can do it for me, of course, he can do it for you.* It's going to change their life.

It's a relief to know our church is full of stories like ours. We're not the only messed up one in a room full of perfect Christ-followers. But what about when it comes to taking our problems to God? He really is perfect. It can feel ridiculous talking about jealousy or unforgiveness with the supreme creator of the universe. What does He care? I'm supposed to open up to Him when I feel like I need to apologize? That sounds so weird. Why would I take this to Him?

In Hebrews 4, the author makes a case for why Jesus is actually the perfect person to be vulnerable with.

> Since then we have a great high priest who has passed through the heavens, Jesus, the Son of God, let us hold fast our confession. For we do not have a high priest who is unable to sympathize with our weaknesses, but one who in every respect has been tempted as we are, yet without sin. (Hebrews 4:14-15)

Jesus, our great high priest, came down to Earth and lived a life like ours. He knows how scary and awful things can be as a human. He's gone through it too. He can sympathize with our weaknesses because He's experienced the same troubles as us.

Have you ever had a friend betray you? So has Jesus.

Have you ever felt like your family didn't believe in you? So has Jesus.

Have you ever felt so weak and alone that you were tempted to give up everything you knew was right for a moment of comfort? So has Jesus.

Have you ever prayed for something to happen, and it didn't happen? So has Jesus. The night before he was arrested, while in the garden praying, Jesus asks God if there was another way. He asked if "this cup could pass." The answer was no. By the end of the night, Jesus accepted it and submitted. But He did pray for it and had to deal with the no.

He's walked this path before us. He is not unsympathetic to our hurts and brokenness. He's been tempted to sin, to lash out in anger, to react selfishly in situations just like ours. He can say, *I've been there too. I know what it's like.*

But what's so great about this passage is that it doesn't leave us there. The author doesn't stop with, *Hey, you can talk to Jesus about how much life sucks because he totally understands.*

Here's the next verse:

> Let us then with confidence draw near to the throne of grace, that we may receive mercy and find grace to help in time of need. (Hebrews 4:16)

141

Because we know that our high priest has been through a life on Earth, we can go BOLDLY to Him for help in time of need.

Not quietly.

Not nervously.

Not waiting until the last minute when things are really bad because we didn't want to bother him with our dumb little problems.

Go boldly as if you're busting through the door to the throne room of heaven. Let it all out.

He will listen. He won't ignore you until you clean yourself up.

He will understand the struggle you are facing because he's lived a life full of temptations.

He will offer you the help you need to get through it.

Who better to offer precisely what you need than someone who has been through it before, and did it perfectly?

If I'm training for a marathon, who am I going to ask to help me? I want someone who had run this race before and succeeded. I want someone who broke records because they did such an amazing job. They're going to know how I should prepare. They'll have the best advice on how not to give up. They know the way!

No one is asking for training tips from the guy who gave up after two miles because he threw up so hard he pooped his pants, then never ran another race. That guy won't be any help at all. Instead, I want the perfect runner, especially after seeing examples of other people he's trained. That makes the runner look even more incredible.

You have a high priest who sympathizes with your weakness and who is ready to help you in times of need. Whenever you start to doubt that, look around your church for examples of others who have gotten the same help you need right now. You're not alone. There's hope.

This is a promise for those who are in Christ. Any comfort that comes from this must be tied to the grace we understand from the last chapter. We don't deserve to approach the throne. We don't deserve to do anything confidently in the presence of God. Yes, Jesus can relate to our experience, but that doesn't make our sin any less evil. His sympathy for us doesn't mean He hears us unload our problems and then say, *Oh yeah that does sound pretty tough. I totally get it. I've been there. Don't feel bad about doing the wrong thing. It's not that big of a deal. Everyone's going to mess that up.*

No.

When you go boldly to the throne, you are speaking to someone with nail scars in his hands. That's why you're even allowed near Him in the first place. It is a gift He paid a heavy price for. Our sin is still sin. Our rebellion against the way of Christ is always wrong and destructive. But in spite of all that He bids us come near. First He came near to us and went through all trials and temptations so He could be our hope. Now we get the benefit of a great high priest who has been here. He will never turn us away. He will never look down on us and dismiss us with, *I don't get what's wrong with you. Try harder.*

He will offer the help you need.

He made Himself the most vulnerable by hanging naked on a cross. He was uncovered, exposed, in the altogether. Even though He was perfect, people still rejected Him. He did it all to make a way so we can be vulnerable with Him.

Go with confidence to Him. You're not the only one who needs to. You're not alone.

## REFLECTION QUESTIONS

How can a Christian be better at using their life as an example, showing others that they are not alone?

How does it make you feel to know that Jesus, in His perfection, is able to sympathize with your difficulties?

What does it look like to you to "boldly go to God?"

# CHAPTER 8

# LITTLE BY LITTLE

*[How We Grow]*

"Nothing can be done except little by little."

Charles Baudelaire

With all this talk about the change that's possible in our lives, we better check in on our expectations.

Salvation comes to those who repent and trust Jesus as Lord. We don't have to work to prove we deserve to follow Him. It's a gift he gives freely and this gift changes everything. We are made new, with a new identity, a new relationship, and a new family.

God relates salvation to adoption, I think that comparison can help us here. When does an orphan become a part of their new family? A judge makes it official by signing all the right paperwork. At that moment, in the eyes of the law, that child is a full-fledged member of the family. All of the rights of any natural child belong to them. That doesn't mean they'll immediately feel like a family the moment the papers are signed. There are going to be some growing pains. It might take a while for everyone to be completely comfortable with this new life. That's OK. Change takes time. The same is true for those of us who are adopted into the family of God. We have all the legal rights of a child, but we're still learning and growing. Not only that we're still becoming more like Jesus.

I wasn't always the best at making that clear.

In 2015 I traveled the country doing a tour of house shows. I posted a video on Facebook saying, "If you can get twenty to thirty people together, I'll come do stand-up in your living room." The video was shared a couple hundred times, and complete strangers started reaching out to book a show.

The tour was a huge success. First of all, I didn't get kidnapped. That's a huge win. My mom was anxious about that. Second, it was unlike anything I had done before. Since a living room was so small and intimate, I designed the show to be half me telling stories and half getting stories from the audience. I'd talk about my first kiss and then ask, "Does anyone have a good first kiss story?" Sometimes I'd get audiences more than happy to take the spotlight and tell their most embarrassing stories. I remember one guy made everyone laugh so hard when he told the story of the first time his wife tried to kiss him. He got up and did a whole ten-minute performance. I just sat back and let him take over the show. It was amazing.

There were also shows where I'd open the floor for stories, and no one would speak up. One time in Arkansas, I asked for first kiss stories, and this woman blurted out, "My first kiss was when I was showing pigs." I was so excited because this sounded like a great story, but when I asked her to elaborate, she said, "We can move on now."

WHAT?!

She just shut me down, refusing to tell the rest of the story. I was FURIOUS. What happened? Was her first kiss with a pig? A rival pig farmer? Did she kiss the judge to get a better score? I never found out.

My house shows were always an hour long, but I'd only bring thirty minutes of material. I knew I could fill the other half with stories from the audience. I wouldn't know what they would be or who they would come from, but I knew I could trust that great stories were waiting to be told.

I called the tour "Tell a Good Story" because I'd end every show with a message on the power of a good story. I wanted the audience to think about the stories in their lives. On the surface, they may look so different, but actually, they all follow the same structure. This was a lesson I learned from Pixar, the film studio behind *Toy Story*, *The Incredibles*, and *Monsters Inc.*

Pixar has rules for storytelling,[1] and one is that all great stories follow the exact same structure.

Once upon a time there was a _____,
everyday they _____, but one day _____,
and everything changed.

You can plug in any famous story.

Once upon a time, there was Cinderella, every day she worked for the evil stepmother and evil stepsisters who treated her like garbage all while she hoped that there could be more to life, but then one day her fairy godmother showed up, and everything changed.

After telling everyone more about my story, I'd show them
the structure.

> Once upon a time, there was Taylor, every day he
> struggled with thoughts and feelings he didn't
> know what to do with. They were killing him on the
> inside and he was too scared to talk about it, but
> then, one day—Jesus—and everything changed.

All of our lives follow the structure too.

At every show, I knew there'd be some people who had a
complete story, one where Jesus came in and changed everything. I wanted them to think about how there were people in
their lives who needed to hear from them, people who needed
to know they weren't alone.

Then I spoke to those in the audience who might not yet
have a complete story, the ones still in the part where every day
they deal with _____, and they're looking for something to
come in and change everything. The truth is we've all tried to
put different things in our stories, hoping it would save us.

When I get out of this town everything is going to change.

*When I get married...*

*When I get a new job...*

*When I just give up and stop caring...*

The only thing that can take over your story and truly
change everything is Jesus.

After performing this in living rooms for a season, I took it
to churches, camps, and conferences. Every once in awhile I'll

still run into people wearing a "Tell a Good Story" shirt. I'm really proud of that time in my life, but looking back, I regret the way I talked about our life stories.

The truth is I oversimplified the story structure Pixar uses. I slimmed it down to better fit my illustration. In reality, what I covered in my show was the structure Pixar used for only the beginning of the story. That's what sets up the rest of the adventure. It's only act one in a three-act story, but the way I told it it was the grand finale. I made it sound like the moment Jesus enters your life, you get a, *And they lived happily ever after.* Once you have Jesus, you won't have to struggle or face any sort of problems ever again. That's just not true. Even in the way I told my story it comes across like the moment I handed my depression over to Jesus, I never dealt with it again. But I did. I still do. There are still times when depression strikes. The difference is now I know what to do when it shows up. I can handle it now because of my Lord and the church.

I still think about the way my oversimplification might have sold a version of salvation that just isn't true. I don't want to make the same mistake with this book.

I'm not even sure I like the way I just described my current relationship with mental health. It's true that now I know what I can do when I'm feeling depressed, but that doesn't mean I always do the right thing. Sometimes it feels like I'm taking two steps forward and one step back. Change isn't always so simple and straightforward. I know it is for some people, but for me, praying a prayer didn't mean everything changed immediately.

I've always been astonished by testimonies where someone shares the exact date and time they were prepared to commit suicide. Their story is about how God met them at that moment, and they never looked back. I'm secretly jealous of those stories. I wish I could point to one specific moment. I wish I could tell you the date of the last time I seriously considered suicide. I don't know. It's all a blur. When I was younger, I wasn't even aware that was what was happening in my brain. The thoughts would go away and come back, looking a little different in each stage of life. It's not like I'm calling for everyone to stop sharing their testimonies if they don't sound exactly like mine. I know some people hit rock bottom, make a decision, and never turn back. But I also want to make room for people like me—the ones who hit rock bottom, make a decision, but do turn back. The ones who fall again. When we only hear one type of story, we can feel like we've missed our one shot at redemption. We think that if it didn't work the first time it's over for us. We're a lost cause. We think, *If I didn't completely change the moment I handed my life over to Jesus, I guess I never will.*

I do have one specific date I can share with you. March 24.

The only reason I know it is because I always write the date with the notes I take at church. During service that Sunday, I was feeling really depressed and a thought about suicide flashed through my mind. It had been a long time since I seriously considered taking my own life. This wasn't like that. This was only a quick thought passing through. I still get one every once in a while. It never stays long. I never make plans. I know it'll pass. At the end of the service, the worship team sang In

Christ Alone, and God used that moment to speak to me. The whole song is beautiful, but the part that really hit me was the line "till he returns or calls me home." The Holy Spirit comforted me with that phrase. I can trust Jesus with my death. He knows my end. He will take me when it's time. He's coming back. This isn't forever. Until that happens, I want to live my life for him. For someone who struggled with the temptation to take his own life, the thought of trusting Jesus with my death was a beautiful reversal of how I used to think. Jesus entered my depression story years ago and changed everything, but I'm still growing, still being transformed, all these years later.

It's still changing. It has taken a lot to get to where I am now, I know there's still a long way to go.

Being in the altogether isn't the one and only fix to all your problems. Making yourself vulnerable is an important step towards change, but it's only the beginning. Remember, your whole life as a Christian is one of progress, growth, and becoming more like Christ. Not all change comes at once.

"Nothing can be done except little by little," said French artist Charles Baudelaire.[2] I know I need to be reminded of this. American culture makes me very impatient.

We can forget how long progress takes in real life because when we see it in a movie, it only takes the length of a song. In a two minute montage you see the hero move to the wilderness, grow a beard, climb a mountain, get super jacked, and discover the all American strength he needs to defeat the evil Russian (name that movie!). Days, weeks, even years can pass in a short movie montage. It all happens so fast. Strangers fall in love, someone learns kung-fu, or the famous musician goes through rehab in no time at all.

BUT THAT'S NOT REAL LIFE!

It's a movie.

They don't show all of the time, effort, work, and heartache that goes into a significant change. That's because movies can't be three hundred hours long. It's not a problem as long as we don't start thinking we can have the same speedy change in real life.

All over the Internet companies are selling a chance to have your own personal movie montage. *Fast fixes! Quick! Lose a hundred lbs in twenty minutes! Get rich by doing absolutely nothing! Be a totally different person by the time your grandma wakes up from her nap!*

But nothing can be done except little by little. Change takes time.

You'll never see Facebook ads like,

"Get over your addiction in seconds flat!"

"Quick and easy steps to get over the death of a loved one."

"Forgive your father for leaving you in no time at all!"

It all happens little by little.

I grew up going to youth camp with my church every year and even though I always had some amazing experiences, it was never the movie montage I wanted. I used to leave camp, thinking I would suddenly have a disciplined prayer life without having to do any real work. I thought everything in my life would just change on its own, and when it didn't, I'd give up.

I'd go back to "normal life" until camp rolled around the next year.

Allowing ourselves to be vulnerable is just the beginning. Talking about our problems doesn't make them go away, it just makes them easier to deal with. There's still a lot of real work to do. Comedian Jacqueline Novak said, "Nothing of merit was ever won without suffering, as we know from Jesus and low-carb diets."[3] Don't get discouraged. Expect the change to happen little by little.

You might feel trapped in a sin and open up to someone about it. The conversation goes really well. They pray with you. You cry. The two of you come up with a plan for how you can follow up over the next few weeks. Later that day, you find yourself falling into that same temptation again. You're so embarrassed. You JUST talked about how you don't want to do this anymore. You feel like you've got to hide this from the person you opened up to because you don't want them to see just how bad things are. You're afraid they're going to change their mind about being there for you. The shame comes on strong, and you're mad at yourself because you literally just read this awesome book that talked about why you shouldn't let shame stop you from reaching out (this one!). You tell yourself, *I should know better.* Don't lose hope.

In the coming weeks, you might feel the need to humble yourself and apologize for something you said in anger. You do the uncomfortable work of owning what you did to show that you want to change. Not long after that conversation, you end up snapping at the person you just apologized to, saying something even worse than before. You're so mad at yourself.

Don't give up.

Don't stop now.

Keep going.

The steps that you take to grow are significant. This will take time, but it's worth it.

I have terrible handwriting. It's so sloppy I get embarrassed when anyone has to read it. I wish I could wave a magic wand and suddenly have amazing penmanship, but that's not how it works.

If I want to change my handwriting, I can only do it one letter at a time. If I go to write my name, at first, I can only focus on making the T as good as it can be. I don't need to worry about any other letters. T is first. Make it perfect. Then comes A, and I just have to put all my effort into making it great. If I do that with every letter for an entire page, at the end, when I zoom out and look at it all together, I will see handwriting that is so much better. Is it perfect? No. But it's improving. It only happens when I focus on one letter at a time. I can't go back and change all the letters that came before this one and I can't get so worried about the letters that are coming later. Can I make the one right in front of me as good as it can be? The handwriting that tells the story of your life can be improved, but I can't promise it will happen overnight.

The first step is being honest about how bad my handwriting is. After that, it's little by little. It's one day at a time. What decision, what step, what act of obedience is in front of me right now?

I heard a psychologist give a lecture where he talked about one of his favorite questions to ask patients dealing with depression: *What are you willing to do to get better?*[4] It's a genius question because it helps you examine your expectations for how things are going to change. A lot of times we want things to change, but we don't want to have to do anything to make the change happen.

Like, I'd love to lose weight. I would love to have abs. Can you picture me with a six-pack? Me neither but I'm sure it would be amazing. I would never wear a shirt. People would be blown away and immediately fall in love with me. My shirtless body does not currently have that effect on people. If I ripped my shirt off in a room of thirty people, two of them would throw up. That's just science.

If I want abs I have to ask myself, *What am I willing to do to make it happen?* Not much. Am I willing to change my diet and stop eating fast food? No. I love how unhealthy my diet is. I could fall asleep eating nachos every night if I had enough money and toilet paper. Am I willing to join a gym so I can have some accountability? When I have to answer that question, it opens my eyes to how little I'm actually willing to do. Then I'm forced to deal with why that is.

What are you willing to do to turn away from sin in your life? Jesus says, "If your right hand causes you to sin, cut it off and throw it away. For it is better that you lose one of your members than that your whole body go into hell." He's not being literal. It's his way of asking, *What are you willing to do?*

Change happens little by little. What are you willing to do to make that change happen? Are you willing to trust God with it? Are you willing to talk about it? Are you willing to cut some things out of your life? Are you willing to see a counselor? Are you willing to join a support group? Are you willing to have that conversation you've been afraid to have for years? Are you willing to keep going even when it feels like nothing good is coming? Are you willing to apologize? Are you willing to do some soul searching and come to terms with why you keep needing to apologize for that thing you keep doing?

Remember that you're not growing and taking steps forward to earn salvation. You're not proving yourself worthy of your relationship with Christ. If you don't grow enough, He's not going to leave you. Salvation is a gift. That change, that adoption is what makes all other changes possible. It frees you to take these steps closer to Jesus.

When Jesus is made Lord of your life, He brings with Him all of the change you could ever hope for. Some change happens all at once the moment you are adopted. Some change is still on its way, but it's coming. The steps you take will lead you to it. It might not be an easy journey straight ahead, but you can celebrate when you take steps forward, not having to lose hope if you end up taking three steps back. You're not the first one on this path. God's grace is not going to run out.

## REFLECTION QUESTIONS

Find some childhood photos of yourself. How have you changed physically, mentally, and spiritually? How did that change occur? If you're going through this book in a small group, you KNOW you have to bring some embarrassing photos to share with everyone.

Write out a goal for yourself. Make it something that you can accomplish, like the illustration of writing a better T. After that, create some more goals, more difficult ones, that would improve your life.

Look at the goals. What are some excuses you have made that have sabotaged your efforts to achieve those goals?

CHAPTER 9

# WHEREVER YOU'RE GOING

*[Comfort for What Comes Next]*

"Immediately the father of the child cried out and said, 'I believe; help my unbelief!'"

Mark 9:24

What if you had to teach someone how to be human?

This is my favorite type of story in TV and film. Something or someone shows up in our world, not knowing how to live in it. The main character finds this thing and has to teach them how to act here. In the first season of Netflix's *Stranger Things*, a group of boys find Eleven, a girl who has lived her entire life in a science facility and has no idea how to be a normal kid. They teach her about waffles and friendship.

I love these stories because of this specific moment that always happens. There's a confrontation because whoever is being taught how to be a human turns out to be better at it than the one teaching because they haven't yet learned how to compromise their beliefs. In *Stranger Things*, Eleven is taught that friends don't lie. She takes it to heart. In her mind, if this is true, then it's ALWAYS true, no matter what. Even when you're scared. Even when you're embarrassed. Then she calls out one of the boys when he tries to lie to her. Why would he lie if "friends don't lie?"

I got obsessed with this idea after watching the show. What if I had to teach someone how to be human? What would I tell them? And how long would it take for them to call me out for being a hypocrite? How long until I don't practice what I preach because I'm too scared to fully commit, and I'd rather take the easy way out? *Didn't you say Christians act like Jesus? Aren't they supposed to love and forgive and have patience?* Maybe they'd call me out for not fully trusting who God says He is. *Isn't God's grace strong enough to cover any sin? Isn't it impossible to make God change His mind about you? Didn't you say we have no reason to hide from Him?* Or maybe they'd call me out for something else entirely. *Didn't you say you were lactose intolerant?! Why are you eating that?!*

We're at the last chapter of the book (I'm going to miss you), and I know throughout everything we've talked about there are a million opportunities for you to compromise. I can't wait for you to find a bald-headed girl with psychic powers to realize any compromises you've made.

Here's what I need you to remember: if it's true, then it's true EVEN FOR YOU.

If it's true that Jesus is a much more trustworthy Lord, then it's true even for you.

If it's true that through Jesus there's hope for change, then it's true even for your situation.

If it's true that opening up is the first step to change, it's true even for you.

If it's true that shame can be defeated when we share it, it's true even for the shame you feel.

If it's true that God speaks a loving **AND YET** to all those who come to Him, it's true even for you. No matter what. No matter how bad things are. No matter what damage you think has been done.

If it's true that the church is full of examples of Christ's perfect patience and that no one is alone in what they're going through, it's true for even you. You're not alone either. Someone has been down in that same hole, and they know the way out.

If it's true that progress happens little by little, it's true for your progress, too.

Don't excuse yourself from the truth. Don't think you're the only exception. Don't leave this book thinking, *That's nice for someone else, but that clearly doesn't apply to me.* If it's true, it's true even for you.

There is hope and grace and community and change waiting for you.

EVEN YOU.

Do you believe it?

Sometimes it feels easier to talk ourselves out of all this stuff, because if it doesn't apply to us, then we never have to make ourselves vulnerable. But when we do that we miss out on so much.

Yes, letting your guard down with someone is a big deal. How will they react? What are they going to say? It's a scary step, but you must take it. Avoiding vulnerability means avoiding the hope for change.

The first time you take that leap of faith is always the scariest. This is why we have to change the way we think about vulnerability. It's not an event, a one time experience we have when we're desperate. It's not meant to be a last resort, saved only for rock bottom. As Christ's followers, our everyday life is meant to be lived depending on our Lord and His church. We don't have it all figured out on our own, so we shouldn't pretend like we do. That leads us to disaster. The road to rock bottom is paved with denial.

Just like the hymn says, we are "prone to wander, Lord, I feel it, prone to leave the God I love." Our sinful nature loves to get us distracted from following Jesus' lead. And this wandering isn't always a dramatic rejection of religion. I know I'm guilty of imagining only an extreme version of wandering so I can feel better about myself. I'll find myself defining wandering as getting a face tattoo of the devil, stealing a cop car, and driving off into the sunset. *Wow, I'm not that bad,* I think, *so I must be good.* But often the wandering is much more subtle. You're not outwardly doing anything horrendous, but you're also not all that concerned with becoming more like Christ. Your faith is "good enough," but the full weight of your trust is not resting on Jesus. You're looking for hope somewhere else. You drift.

I wonder how much of our drifting starts because we wanted to avoid a vulnerable moment. We should have apologized. We need to confront someone. We were afraid to talk about our dreams. We didn't know how to open up about a tragedy or when a sin showed back up in our lives. The way shame can pull you back into hiding doesn't have to be drastic. You might not even notice it's happening. It could feel more like a slow drift. Little by little, you take back some of the trust you put in Jesus. He wanted you to be open and vulnerable, but you didn't think that was necessary, so you went a different way. It's not just progress that happens little by little, it's how things fall apart too.

My point is, why wait for rock bottom? Why let yourself drift off from God and never notice until things come crashing down? There's no guarantee that'll be the wake up call you need to finally come out of hiding. Instead, if we practice vulnerability in our everyday lives, we'll have a safety net to catch us when we are most prone to wander.

The Holy Spirit might already be nudging you about things in your life you need to trust Him with. You know there's hope waiting for you. You know His grace is enough and there's nothing that will make Him change His mind about you. You know you're not alone, not the first one to be in this position. You know all that, but there's still some fear. I understand. It's risky to let your guard down.

There's one important aspect of God's character that can comfort us as we take that leap of faith: wherever you're going, God's already there. It's a theme all throughout scripture.

In Judges 7, God calls Gideon to raise up an army for battle. Gideon is terrified. He knows he's not qualified as a leader. He knows the enemy's army is much bigger and stronger than his. In Gideon's mind, there's no way he'll win. The night before the battle, an angel of the Lord appears and instructs him to sneak down to the enemy's camp and eavesdrop on the soldiers. This is what happens:

> When Gideon came, behold, a man was telling a dream to his comrade. And he said, "Behold, I dreamed a dream, and behold, a cake of barley

bread tumbled into the camp of Midian and came to the tent and struck it so that it fell and turned it upside down, so that the tent lay flat." And his comrade answered, "This is no other than the sword of Gideon the son of Joash, a man of Israel; God has given into his hand Midian and all the camp."

As soon as Gideon heard the telling of the dream and its interpretation, he worshiped. And he returned to the camp of Israel and said, "Arise, for the Lord has given the host of Midian into your hand." (Judges 7:13-15)

Not only does God want Gideon to see that He's going into battle with him, God also shows Gideon He's already working in the enemy's camp, preparing them for their defeat. God gives this soldier a prophetic dream about how Gideon will defeat them JUST SO Gideon can overhear him talking about it. It's a sign of confirmation. God is saying, *I'm already here! You can trust me. I'm already at work where I'm sending you.* He does this over and over in scripture.

When the Israelites enter the promised land, God commands them to conquer the existing cities and establish their own kingdom. The Israelites are not equipped to be mighty in battle. They have very little faith in their own abilities, but to their surprise, when spies are sent into a city to scope things out, they meet someone who basically says, *Oh we've been waiting for you. We've heard Israel is coming. We've known God is on your side, and you're going to take us over. We've just been waiting around for that to happen.* God was already there.

We can see this with Jesus too. Before His ministry, John the Baptist was called to "prepare the way of the Lord." Even with Jesus, God doesn't send Him out into the unknown alone. He sends someone to go ahead.

In Acts 19, Christ appears to Saul on the road to Damascus and tells him to stop persecuting Christians. Saul is blinded by the vision and totally humbled by the realization that Jesus really is who his followers say he is, the son of God. He's ready to change his life and follow his new Lord. Jesus instructs him to find a man named Ananias in a nearby town, who'll be able to heal Saul's blindness and disciple him. We also get to read Ananias' side of the story. Jesus appears to him and says something like, *Hey, you know that Saul guy who keeps killing Christians? Well, he's in some trouble, and I need you to take care of him.* Ananias is not on board. He doesn't even want to be in the same room as Saul because he's afraid of what he'll do to him.

What do you think Saul was thought when God told him to go to this Christian? It was probably just like how Ananias felt. *Why would this guy ever help me? Christians must hate me. There's no way I'll be able to go to him for help.* Neither of them knew that God was already with the other one, preparing them for their encounter.

It's throuhout scripture. Wherever God is sending you, he's already there.

Do you feel like God is calling you to get involved in ministry, but you're nervous about taking that step? He's already preparing a spot for you.

Are you in Ananias' shoes and God has laid someone on your heart? You're scared to share the gospel with them because you've heard how they talk about religion? God is already with them, preparing them for that conversation.

Are you a Saul right now? You know you've been avoiding being vulnerable and you feel like God is pulling you to open up to someone you trust. Right now, it feels impossible. Take comfort in the character of God. Look at this consistent pattern throughout scripture. If He's leading you somewhere, He's not sending you alone. Not only is He going with you, but He's already there, preparing the way.

He's with your spouse.

He's with your pastor.

He's in the counselor's office.

He's already at that moment, and we can trust that it's safe for us to join Him there.

Is it still a leap of faith? Yes.

Does this mean everything will always be super easy because He prepared the way? I really wish it did. But sadly, it can still get messy. We can still get hurt. There's a lot of real work that comes after opening up. I can't guarantee the person you open up to will handle it perfectly.

But He's still with you.

Do you feel that tug on your heart? Maybe the Holy Spirit shined a spotlight on that one issue, and you feel the pull to find someone to open up to about it. Maybe the Holy Spirit opened your eyes to see the smaller everyday moments you can be vulnerable with. Trust that it's the right thing to do. Pray for whoever it is you're trusting with that vulnerable moment.

Pray for wisdom and patience.

Pray for the right opportunity to present itself for you two to talk.

It can be pretty scary. It's OK to admit that. But take comfort in knowing that if it's the path God wants you to walk, He's with you, and He's already ahead of you, preparing the way.

God might also be preparing you for someone else's vulnerable conversation. A perfect moment might present itself, and someone could be opening up to you. Honestly, that can be just as intimidating as being the one who needs to share. But there's nothing to be afraid of. Offer them all the things you hope someone would give you when you open up. Show grace. Let them know they're not alone. Remember that change happens little by little, so you don't have to worry about saying the perfect thing that'll fix all their problems in an instant.

If we can create a culture in the church where Christians are comfortable on both sides of a vulnerable conversation, it will be an incredible witness to a world without hope. We can make that happen, little by little, and we can trust that God is already ahead of us, preparing the way.

Something good is coming.

## REFLECTION QUESTIONS

In what areas have you noticed "the drift?" Think about how and where it began. What are some specific ways you could course correct?

Write down the names of two people with whom you could be vulnerable. When is a time you could get-together where being vulnerable will be a component of the interaction?

How does it feel knowing God is already wherever He is sending you?

Take a moment and pray that God would prepare you to receive someone else's vulnerability. How do you want to respond?

# ACKNOWLEDGEMENTS

I acknowledge that Jesus is the son of God. I acknowledge the earth is round. I acknowledge that writing a book is really really really hard, and there are a lot of people who helped make this thing possible. I would like to thank them now.

My parents, Alan and Gina Johnson, have supported in incredibly ways, in every season of my life, except when I told them I didn't want to go to college. I mean, they still supported me, but they weren't too excited at first.

When I was younger Glyndon Greer taught me how to talk to God. Now he's helping me live out the things I think God is calling me to do. This book would not exist without him.

Garland Owensby is the one who showed me how comedy could be used for ministry. I've looked to him for guidance and encouragement every step of the way.

Several people read early drafts of the book. Their feedback helped shape it into something stronger than I could have ever made on my own. Cameron Combs, Michah Carney, Weston Combs, Chelsea Barrera, Dani Barrera, Cait Barrera, Tim Enloe, Wade Bearden, Emily Oakley, and Zena Carter.

Joseph Urbina also read an earlier draft but I felt he deserved to be singled out because of the hours he spent helping me not sound like a total idiot. His grammar and formatting notes (there were A LOT) actually makes this thing read good. Can you tell he didn't edit this section?

I also need to thank everyone who has ever supported me financially through Patreon. Wade & Priscilla Bearden, Ministry Pass, Justin Jonker, Christopher Bejarano, Holly Matherne, Chance Abbott, Heather Benavides, Gary Lankford, David and Whitnye Hale, Jaclyn and Rick Hinojosa, Dallin Malmgren, Vickey Ward, Karen Sponseller, Joel Piercy, Anali Regaldo Galvan, Cameron and Katie Ward, Chris Fleniken, Lisa and Ron Davis, Joe Franklin, Creighton Coleman, Derek Fults, Jerame Edwards, Jessika Martinez, Ferris Polk, Angie Newkirk, Beverly Robinson, Garland Owensby, Stacey G. Bunn, Sidney Prado, Hannah Barnes, Debbie Stocks, Jerry Griffin, Melissa Vasilie, Natalie M, Andrew Maniaici Adam Shelton, Tyler Harris, Michelle Paul, Cameron Combs, Kent Kirby, Faith Orcutt, Natassia McIntosh, CJ McDaniel, Manny Alvarez, Khris Graves, Laban Massey, Cassie Pate, Pamela Young, Stephanie Cardenas.

# NOTES

## CHAPTER ONE

1. Susan Cain. "The Power of Introverts." TED Talk, www.ted.-com/talks/susan_cain_the_power_of_introverts?language=en.

## CHAPTER TWO

1. Andrew Peterson. "God's Faithfulness in Andrew Peterson's Weakness." The Gospel Coalition, www.thegospelcoalition.org/video/gods-faithfulness-andrew-petersons-weakness/.

## CHAPTER THREE

1. Deborah Farmer Kris. "The Timeless Teachings of Mister Rogers." PBS Kids for Parents, 20 Mar. 2017, www.pbs.org/parents/thrive/the-timeless-teachings-of-mister-rogers.

2. "You're Only as Sick as Your Secrets." Sound Recovery Solutions, soundrecoverysolutions.com/sick-as-secrets/.

3. I go to The Oaks Church in Red Oak, TX and my pastor is Scott Wilson. I can't pinpoint one specific sermon where he used this illustration. I've heard him say it several times. I don't really know how best to cite this source. I probably could have just lied and pretended I came up with it and no one would have noticed. He's not going to read this. But at the same time I really hate when people don't credit their sources.

4. Josh Larsen. Movies Are Prayers: How Films Voice Our Deepest Longings. InterVarsity Press, 2017. Pg. 99

## CHAPTER FOUR

1. Joshua Harris. Statement on "I Kissed Dating Goodbye". joshharris.com/statement/.

2. Joshua Harris. Strong Enough to Be Wrong. www.youtube.com/watch?v=D2kV4ngi7J4

3. Charles Duhigg. "Episode 2: Telling the Truth." *Change Agent*, 6 Aug. 2018, www.nytimes.com/2018/08/06/podcasts/change-agent-telling-the-truth.html?action=click&module=audio-series-bar®ion=header&pgtype=Article.

4. Megan Mccluskey. "Dan Harmon Gives 'Full Account' of Sexually Harassing Community Writer Megan Ganz." *Time*, 11 Jan. 2018, time.com/5100019/dan-harmon-megan-ganz-sexual-harassment-apology/.

5. Ibid

# CHAPTER FIVE

1. Jon Ronson. So You've Been Publicly Shamed. Riverhead Books, 2015. Pg. 31

2. Brene Brown. *The Power of Vulnerability*. www.youtube.com/watch?v=iCvmsMzlF7o.

3. Vivek Murthy. "Work and the Loneliness Epidemic." *Harvard Business Review*, hbr.org/cover-story/2017/09/work-and-the-loneliness-epidemic.

4. Jonathan Franzen. *Farther Away*. Fourth Estate, 2013. Pg. 7

5. Keller, Timothy, and Kathy Keller. The Meaning of Marriage: Facing the Complexities of Commitment with the Wisdom of God. Penguin Books, 2013. Pg. 95

6. Brene Brown. The Gifts of Imperfection. Hazelden Publishing, 2015. Pg. 10

# CHAPTER SIX

1 All of the quotes from this story can be found in John 4:7-39

# CHAPTER SEVEN

1 Charles Duhigg. The Power of Habit: Why We Do What We Do in Life and Business. Random House Trade Paperbacks, 2014. Pg. 85

# CHAPTER EIGHT

1. Cyriaque Lamar. "The 22 Rules of Storytelling, According to Pixar." *Gizmodo*, 8 June 2012, io9.gizmodo.com/the-22-rules-of-storytelling-according-to-pixar-5916970.

2. Will Gompertz. What Are You Looking At? Plume Books, 2013. Pg. 32

3. Jacqueline Novak. How to Weep in Public: Feeble Offerings on Depression From One Who Knows. Three Rivers Press, 2016. Pg. 167

4. This is a Jordan Peterson quote. To be honest, I didn't want to credit him in the text of the chapter because of his new found role in pop culture as a polarizing figure. My fear was that bringing up his name brought along a ton of baggage and assumptions, whether you like the guy or hate him. I wanted to let the quote live on its own, apart from his reputation and potential controversy. It's good, right? I found it a couple years before he started turning up in headlines.

# ABOUT THE AUTHOR

Taylor Johnson is a comedian, speaker, and now an author living in Dallas, TX. For almost a decade he has ended his stand-up shows with a message on vulnerability.

His honesty and humor can disarm audiences and create a safe environment where people feel comfortable opening up about the realities and difficulties of their lives.

# FOLLOW TAYLOR

Want more? Sign up for Taylor Johnson's weekly newsletter. Every Monday morning you'll get jokes, stories, resources, recommendations, and exclusive offers.

FollowTaylor.com

Made in the USA
Columbia, SC
06 December 2019